RYA Boat Safet

CW00546997

© Keith Colwell/RYA
First Published 2012
The Royal Yachting Association
RYA House, Ensign Way, Hamble
Southampton SO31 4YA
Tel: 0844 556 9555
Fax: 0844 556 9516
E-mail: publications@rya.org.uk
Web: www.rya.org.uk
ISBN: 978-1-906435530
RYA Order Code: G103

Totally Chlorine
Free

Sustainable
Forests

Note: While all reasonable care has been taken in the preparation
of this book, the publisher takes no responsibility for the use of the
methods or products or contracts described in the book.

Cover Design: Design House
Illustrations: Steve Lucas
Typeset: KJS Design
Proofreading and indexing: Alan Thatcher
Printed in China through World Print
Acknowledgement: Sara Hopkinson

CONTENTS

INTRODUCTION

'An ounce of prevention is worth a pound of cure'

Some say it was Benjamin Franklin, scientist and the eldest founding father of the USA who coined this phrase. Others claim it dates back to the reign of Henry III. Whoever it was, they surely must have been a yachtsman since these words are so apt for anyone who takes a boat to sea.

While some might justifiably worry about today's blame culture society, where lawyers hunt for those looking for legal retribution against errant owners, others inherently know that proper preparation is part of the duty of care they have to their boat and crew. They understand that, when the chips are down, being found wanting of a vital piece of gear can make the difference between making a safe landing or not.

Of course, it's not equipment alone that makes for a safe little ship. Safety is as much to do with an attitude of mind – brought about by proper training – as it is about, say, fitting the right size anchor. It's a core value of the RYA and should be in the mind of every skipper and crew. Not only because it makes boating safer but also because knowing what you are doing, and doing it well, makes going afloat more enjoyable.

But with the knowledge that comes from training, it soon becomes apparent that to take to the water without the right equipment is to fail to understand what you have learnt.

This book builds on many people's years of experience of choosing the right gear to safely go afloat. We will never stop dire accidents from happening. But proper preparation can, and does, prevent the lesser problems and will, at least, ameliorate the major ones to improve significantly our chances of survival.

Chapter 1 What do you Need to go Afloat Safely?

So you've bought your boat but is she ready to go to sea? If she's a new boat then probably not since, even with the introduction of the Recreational Craft Directive (page 22) the 'essential equipment' supplied with the boat will not include personal safety items, relevant charts and pilot books, throwing lines, appropriate radio equipment or indeed a host of other safety gear necessary for your type of boating.

To be fair, it would be an impossible task for a boat builder to put together the perfect pack since each boat owner will have their personal preferences on the equipment they want for their boat. For boats of 13.7m in length and over certain minimum carriage requirements are set out in Merchant Shipping Regulations (see page 16) and these requirements are often used as guidance by the owners of boats less than 13.7m in length. Even when buying a used boat, take your time to go through what you have on board and assess what else you will need.

What equipment you need will, of course, depend on how the boat is to be used. You may own a RCD Category A vessel but that doesn't mean to say you will be using it to cross oceans. Consequently, there is no need to fit the boat out to trans-ocean standards if you only ever plan to use it for coastal passages.

Conversely, there are numerous examples of sailors who have taken small craft far beyond their expected cruising areas. One only has to read of the exploits of Hugo Vihlen, Tom McClean and Tom McNally in their attempts to cross the Atlantic in yachts smaller than most people's dinghies to realise that ocean sailing is not just the preserve of 'ocean-going' yachts. And it's not only sail boats that undertake Atlantic and Round the World challenges. Alan Priddy and his team took their 33ft (10m) RIB *Spirit of Cardiff* on several trans-ocean challenges.

There are plenty of examples of more normal small craft sailing oceans. When Francis Chichester and Blondie Hasler set up the OSTAR (Observer Single Handed Trans-Atlantic Race) in 1960, they set the lower size limit at just 25ft (7.6m). Hasler himself crossed in *Jester*, a modified version of a 25ft Folkboat.

Notable cruising sailors from the Hiscocks to the Pardeys, have all sailed the world in craft under 30ft (9m). While in the Seventies, small boat yachtsman Shane Acton took *Shrimpy*, his 18ft (6m) bilge-keel Caprice sailing boat, round the world. It's unlikely any would be officially classed as ocean-going vessels today.

The common factor with all these sailors is the thorough preparation their skippers undertook to ensure safe passage coupled with good seamanship and, it has to be said, sometimes remarkable good luck.

Accepting that there are exceptions, as a general guideline for the rest of us more moderate boat users, unless you have the experience, knowledge and ability, it makes sense to stay within the capabilities of your craft and crew.

To help you decide on what you will first need, you need to consider how you intend to use your boat, i.e. its intended area of operation. The Small Commercial Vessel and Pilot Boat (SCV) Code gives a good basis for this.

While the SCV has seven categories, this has been reduced to four since the differences in equipment recommended for a vessel that is travelling up to 150 miles offshore and 60 miles offshore is minimal. Similarly, while the code reduces its requirements for vessels used within 20 miles of a safe haven if used in favourable weather and in daylight, our list takes the pragmatic approach that it may simply not be possible to avoid bad weather or to ensure return before nightfall and therefore it is better to err on the side of caution and provide the same advice for all craft up to 20 miles from a safe haven.

There are, of course, no firm boundaries at sea and one needs to accept that any recommendations are only guidelines.

Boats and their area of operation

Unrestricted
Vessels that make long distance passages capable of withstanding heavy storms and able to meet serious emergencies without outside help. Boats are expected to be self sufficient in the event of an accident and, in case of emergency, carry enough equipment and spares to take care of themselves for possibly a considerable length of time until help arrives. The boat should have sufficient resources to undertake repairs that allow it to make its own way towards a safe haven or rescue.

Up to 60 miles from shore and a safe haven
Vessels that make offshore passages and capable of withstanding heavy weather conditions but able to make their way to a safe haven within 12 hours. Boats should be self sufficient with a provision of equipment suitable for the expected sea conditions. The boat should have sufficient resources to undertake repairs that allow it to make its own way towards a safe haven or rescue.

Up to 20 miles from shore and a safe haven
Vessels that cruise along the coast and up to 20 miles from the shore during daylight and night hours. The boat should be able to withstand moderately bad weather conditions and capable of making their way to a safe haven within four hours. They should have sufficient resources to provide a significant degree of self sufficiency to allow time in an emergency for help to arrive and have sufficient resources to undertake repairs that allow it to make its own way towards a safe haven or rescue.

Up to 3 miles from shore
Vessels that are suitable for protected waters, in favourable weather and daylight, where effective rescue is close at hand. A boat should have sufficient resources to allow it to make its own way towards a safe anchorage, landing or rescue.

Stability

When considering the suitability of your boat for a particular voyage, you should take into account its stability and seaworthiness. Due to the RCD, boats built or put into service since 1998 within the European Economic Area are required to meet ISO 12217. Sailing yachts in categories A and B are provided with a GZ curve and a STIX (STability IndeX) number. These details give an indication of the boat's stability and seaworthiness.

Stability (GZ) curve

For a boat to float, its weight has to be supported by its buoyancy. The amount of upward force holding the boat afloat will be equal to the boat's displacement (or weight). Its weight can be considered to be acting through one point – the boat's centre of gravity and the upward force of buoyancy can also be considered to be acting through one point, its centre of buoyancy.

When a vessel is upright, the centre of gravity (CG) will be on the same vertical line as the centre of buoyancy (CB). When a boat is heeled due to an outside force such as the wind or waves, the CG stays in the same position but the CB moves sideways in the direction the boat is heeled. There's now a turning moment with the weight of the boat acting down through the CG and the buoyancy of the boat acting upwards through the CB. The forces are trying to bring the boat back to the upright position.

The distance between the line of force acting downwards through the CG and the line of force acting upwards through the CB is known as GZ.

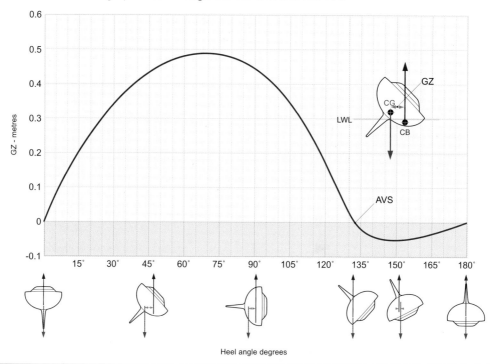

As the boat heels further the GZ increases until it reaches its maximum and then slowly decreases as the boat goes over on to its side and beyond. So long as the value of GZ is above zero then if the capsizing force is removed the boat will return to upright. The point where the CG and CB are again in line is called the Angle of Vanishing Stability (AVS). If the boat heels further it will turn turtle and remain inverted unless an outside force or the action of the waves forces it back up again.

In sailing yachts, the AVS can vary from as little as 90 degrees up to 155 degrees. Vessels with high cabins or a pilot house may even be self-righting – assuming the cabin windows and hatches remain watertight.

The amount of the righting moment is a product of the length of the GZ and the boat's mass – the larger the GZ and the greater the mass of the boat, the greater the righting moment and the greater the ability of the boat to withstand outside forces.

For a sailing yacht to qualify for one of the four RCD categories, under ISO 12217-2, it has to have a minimum AVS and, in the case of cat A and B a minimum displacement – see the table below.

Ballasted monohull-yacht stability indicators				
Design category	A	B	C	D
Typical wind force (Beaufort)	Up to 10	Up to 8	Up to 6	Up to 4
Wind gusts up to m/s (knots)	28 (54)	21 (41)	17 (33)	13 (25)
Wave height up to…	Approx 7m*	4m*	2m*	0.5 max
Displacement – m/kg	>3000	>1500kg	No limit	No limit
Minimum AVS (degree)	130 – 0.002m	130 – 0.005m	90	75
but never less than (degree)	100	95	90	75
Minimum STIX	32	23	14	5

* significant wave height (the mean height of the highest one-third of the waves, which approximately corresponds to the wave height estimated by an experienced observer. Some waves will be double this height.

As an example of the sort of figures that can be expected, the Contessa 32 has a STIX of 33 and an AVS of 133 degrees while the STIX for the Melges 24 is 15 with an AVS of 130 degrees.

Melges 24
Fiona Brown

The higher the STIX number, the more able the yacht is to take on heavy weather.

The RYA provide a continually updated Stability List for over 400 boats in the Regulations & Safety section of its website. Also, see the RYA publication G23 RYA Stability and Buoyancy.

Adding weight aloft

On sail boats, while adding a relatively small amount of extra weight aloft, such as radar antenna or roller furling gear for the headsail, will make little difference in the boat's overall displacement (weight), it can have a significant effect to the yacht's GZ when the boat is heeled and reduce the boat's angle of vanishing stability. Seek advice from the RYA's technical department.

Similarly on a motor boat take care not to overload a flying bridge with too many passengers and crew.

Sailing yacht seaworthiness factor

While a stability curve provides a good indication of a boat's static stability, it does not give the full picture. The ISO 12217 working group developed a further screen as a measure of a ballasted monohull sailing yacht's dynamic stability, or comparative sea worthiness, called STIX. STIX rates yachts on a scale of 1 to 100, based on its length and seven other factors…

- Ability to withstand a capsize by considering the area under its GZ curve

- Recovery from inversion by comparing its AVS and displacement

- Recovery from knockdown by overcoming water in the sails

- Displacement/length factor – with credit for heavy displacement for a given length

- Beam/displacement factor which takes into consideration problems associated with topside flare and wide beam

- The risk of downflooding in a knockdown

- Wind moment representing the risk of flooding due to a gust

Motorboats

Larger motorboats will also have had the required stability calculations undertaken but these are not usually published in the owner's manual. Ask the builder or supplier.

Loading conditions will be provided and, as with all craft, motorboats should not be overloaded – particularly smaller power craft which are more susceptible to swamping.

Motorboats will also have had calculated the angle of heel at which downflooding will occur. Downflooding is the term used for water flooding over the edge of the cockpit and into the boat.

Chapter 2: Rules and Regulations for Non-Commercial Pleasure Craft

In the UK boats classified under the Merchant Shipping Regulations as pleasure vessels are relatively unregulated, although these are a few guiding regulations. Some apply to all boats, some depend on the size of boat and some on how and where you use your boat.

What is a pleasure vessel?

Under the Merchant Shipping Regulations, a pleasure vessel is defined as a vessel used for sport or recreational purposes only by its owner (or the immediate family or friends of the owner) and does not operate for any financial gain to the owner or anyone else. If the boat is owned by a corporate body, the users of the boat can be the organisation's officers or employees or their immediate family or friends.

The owner must not receive money for, or in connection with, operating the vessel or carrying any person other than as a contribution to the direct expenses of the operation of the vessel incurred during the voyage or excursion.

Vessels owned by, or on behalf of, a members' club formed for the purpose of sport or pleasure also fall into this category so long as any charges levied are paid into club funds and applied to the general use of the club. This allows clubs who, for example, use a boat as a club taxi to ferry members out to their boats on moorings, to ask for a payment towards fuel and maintenance of the taxi without fear of it being classed as a commercial vessel.

No more than 12 passengers

Recreational boat owners also need to take heed of the number of 'passengers' carried aboard their boat. If more than 12 passengers are carried, whether as paying passengers or not, the boat will be regarded as a 'passenger ship' and therefore subject to the Merchant Shipping Regulations applicable to such vessels. A passenger is considered to be anyone who is not engaged in the running of the boat.

While on smaller boats, the physical constraints of the boat make it virtually impossible, undesirable and even darned uncomfortable to take on board that many people, it's easily achievable on larger boats. So the owner/skipper of a large motor cruiser will need to limit their largesse when inviting all their friends aboard for a trip round the bay.

Thankfully, there is a proviso, where common sense prevails, that allows the limit to be broken when taking aboard survivors or others in distress. Curiously, under the Regulations, a child under the age of one is not considered to be a passenger.

SOLAS

The International Convention of Safety of Life at Sea (SOLAS) has been in force for merchant ships since 1914. Fire fighting equipment and lifesaving appliances have been required for pleasure vessels over 13.7m in length since at least the 1960s. SOLAS has been developed and extended throughout the century but it wasn't until July 2002 that SOLAS Chapter V (Safety of Navigation) was revised to include pleasure craft. Shown below are the SOLAS V regulations that are applicable to pleasure craft and notes on how they affect us. Some show the exact wording (italics) while others have been paraphrased for brevity.

Radar reflector – Regulation 19.2.1.7

All ships shall have, if less than 150 gross registered tonnes and if practicable, a radar reflector or other means, to enable detection by ships navigating by radar at both 9 and 3GHz.

■ 'When practicable' means that if your boat can carry a radar reflector, you should. Both passive radar reflectors and active devices (radar target enhancers) are available – there are advantages and disadvantages to both types. In 2006 the Maritime and Coastguard Agency (MCA) issued a guidance note that suggested that in addition to having a radar reflector aboard it should be hoisted (or switched on) at all times. For more details on the types and applications of radar reflectors see page 58.

Lifesaving signals – Regulation 29

An illustrated table describing the life-saving signals shall be readily available to the officer of the watch on every ship to which this chapter applies. The signals shall be used by ships or persons in distress when communicating with life-saving stations, maritime rescue units and aircraft engaged in SAR ops.

■ To comply with this regulation, you will need to carry a copy of the table on board. Since it is included in a number of marine publications, including inside most almanacs and on the back of some Admiralty charts, there's a good chance you will already have this onboard.
http://www.direct.gov.uk/en/TravelAndTransport/Boatingandtravellingbywater/
Usingpleasurecraftsafely/DG_185461

Danger messages – Regulation 31

Masters are to communicate information on navigational dangers. These include, for example, a dangerous derelict or other dangerous obstructions, tropical storms, winds of Force 10 or more for which no warning has been received. The form that information is sent is not obligatory and it can be transmitted in plain language or using the International Code of Signals. Contracting governments must promulgate any danger information received and messages must be free to ships.

■ This means that you, as skipper, have a duty to pass on information about navigational dangers, to the Coastguard and shipping.

Information required in danger messages – Regulation 32

Regulation 32 provides guidance as to what to include in a danger message. It covers details on ice, sub-freezing air temperatures, derelicts, tropical cyclones and winds of Force 10 or above for which no storm warning has been received. The recommended details are those which any prudent navigator would wish to to know. For example: the kind of ice, derelict or danger observed, its position and the time and date (Universal Co-ordinated Time (UTC)) when the danger was last observed.

The Regulation requires the Master to report any encounter with Force 10 or more winds or tropical storms. This obligation should be interpreted in broad spirit, and information transmitted whenever the Master has good reason to believe that a tropical cyclone is developing or exists in the neighbourhood. Details should include time, date (UTC) and position of the ship when the observation was taken. Observations should include barometric pressure, pressure tendency, true wind direction and strength (Beaufort scale), state of the sea (smooth, moderate, rough, high), the direction, size and period of swell and the true course and speed of the ship. Although it's not obligatory, Reg. 32 also asks that observations are made and transmitted hourly, if practicable – or at least every three hours – for as long as the ship is in the storm.

Sub-freezing air temperatures associated with gale force winds can cause severe amounts of ice to form on superstructures, masts and rigging and, as with tropical storms, information such as time, date, air temperature, sea temperature and wind force and direction should be reported.

Distress Messages: Obligations and procedures – Regulation 33

Enshrined into SOLAS V is the long-held maritime principle of helping fellow seafarers in distress at sea.

The master of a ship at sea which is in a position to be able to provide assistance on receiving a signal from any source that persons are in distress at sea, is bound to proceed with all speed to their assistance, if possible informing them or the search and rescue service that the ship is doing so. If the ship receiving the distress alert is unable or, in the special circumstances of the case, considers it unreasonable or unnecessary to proceed to their assistance, the master must enter in the log-book the reason for failing to proceed to the assistance of the persons in distress, taking into account the recommendation of the Organization, to inform the appropriate search and rescue service accordingly.

■ Not only does Regulation 33 make it, if practicable, a requirement to provide assistance but also, if need be, to pass on a distress message to the Search and Rescue (SAR) authorities. What's more, Regulation 33 also allows the Master of the vessel in distress or the SAR authorities (after consultation) to requisition other ships to provide assistance with all speed to the persons in distress. In other words, it's not only your moral duty to assist but your legal duty as well.

Safe navigation and avoidance of dangerous situations – Regulation 34

Voyage planning is required on all vessels that go to sea. 'Going to sea' is defined as proceeding outside of categorised waters. You can get more information about what constitutes categorised waters from the MCA and RYA. MSN 1827 is available from the MCA website.

MCA guidance notes say for 'small craft and pleasure vessels, the degree of voyage planning will be dependant on the size of the vessel, its crew and the length of the voyage'. The MCA says that it 'expects all mariners to make a careful assessment of any proposed voyage taking into account all dangers to navigation, weather forecasts, tidal predictions and other relevant factors including the competence of the crew'.

■ This regulation makes it a requirement for all skippers to undertake a voyage or passage plan before departure, however far their trip. There's no suggested set format and it does not have to be written down.

■ It's difficult to provide firm guidelines but it's reasonable to expect that boats on more than a day trip 'around the bay' to have a written log showing they have made the appropriate preparations in checking the weather forecasts and tidal predictions and to have plotted the route on a recognised chart and made contingency plans in case of an emergency. Even if you are on a day trip 'around the bay', you should still plan appropriately, taking into account your familiarity with the area and the conditions you may face.

■ Whether on a short or long trip, you should have a chart on board and be aware of the navigational dangers and have checked the weather forecast and tidal predictions for the area and be sure that they fit in with your planned trip.

■ RYA practical courses provide students with the ability to create an acceptable and useable passage plan.

■ Skippers also need to take into account the limitations of their vessel and the experience and physical ability of their crew – are they able to cope with the length of the voyage and the expected conditions? Could the crew take over command should the skipper become ill or fall overboard?

■ Part of the voyage plan should be letting a competent person ashore know your plans and what to do should they become concerned about your wellbeing. The MCA recommend taking advantage of their Voluntary Safety Identification Scheme, best known as CG66 (see page 154).

All voyage plans should include checking the weather forecast and tidal predictions for the area you plan to sail. Weather information is now widely available from a number of sources including Navtex, VHF, the internet, radio and TV.

Tidal data including range and current direction is also widely available. Strong tidal flows should be taken into consideration when planning your voyage since strong currents will not only alter your speed but also may affect the sea conditions.

For more information on voyage planning see G69 RYA Passage Planning.

Keeping a Log

It is good practice to keep a log, especially when out of sight of land. All UK vessels on international voyages (other than pleasure vessels of less than 150grt) must keep on board a record of navigational activities so their passage can be reconstructed. For pleasure vessels under 150grt there are no specific requirements, although the RYA encourages all to maintain a detailed log.

Harbour Authority Byelaws and Regulations

Harbour Authorities normally put in place Byelaws to regulate vessels' movement and support safe navigation. The byelaws can be extensive and include speed limits, restrictions on waterskiing, personal watercraft, wind and kite surfers, the use of vessels under the influence of drink and drugs. In some harbours, the Authorities may even have the power to prevent craft from going to sea if not properly and safely fitted out.

Harbour Authorities will provide printed copies of their Byelaws and details are often provided in almanacs and pilot books. Many harbours now also have websites where details of the byelaws and the harbourmasters' directions are also provided. Check what's required of your home port and those that you plan to visit.

Pollution & Rubbish

The International Convention for the Prevention of Pollution from Ships 1973 modified by the Protocol of 1978 is better known as MARPOL 73/78. It does not apply to small craft carrying fewer than 15 passengers but nevertheless makes good sense whatever the size and capacity of the vessel. In brief, it says that no waste should be put over the side under any circumstances. Vessels over 12m are obliged to have information about MARPOL regulations on board.

An EU directive supports the Convention and now insists that all vessels have to put waste into a waste reception facility before leaving port, unless they can carry it all to their next port of call. Some European countries also now preclude the use of sea toilets while in port and in coastal waters. Any sewage discharge into inland waterways is offensive and against the law on most. Pleasure vessel owners and skippers should be aware that they are required to comply with regulations 26–28, 30 and 31 of the Merchant Shipping (Prevention of Pollution by Sewage and Garbage from Ships) Regulations 2008. The basic principle is to not put any garbage into the sea; garbage should be retained on board and disposed of ashore. Garbage means all food, domestic and operational wastes produced on board (except sewage) although food wastes may be disposed of at sea if they have been pulverised and you are at least 3 miles offshore (this is extended to 12 miles offshore in the North Sea or English Channel).

For vessels whose length overall is 12 metres or more, regulation 31 requires placards notifying the crew and passengers of regulations 26–28 and 30 (which places restrictions on vessels entering the Antarctic Area) to be displayed. The Green Blue also offers best practice advice to boaters about minimising their impact on the environment.

International Regulations for Preventing Collisions at Sea

Better known by many as the Colregs, the regulations provide the framework for the safe navigations of vessels at sea. As well as providing the 'rules of the road', the IRPCS also give the requirements for navigation lights, day shapes, sound signals and distress signals for all craft including boats. Details of the lights, shapes and sound signals to use on small craft are shown on pages 96, 102 and 103.

....
■ The full text of the regulations is available in the RYA publication RYA G2 – International Regulations for Preventing Collisions at Sea.
....

UK Merchant Shipping Regulations (Class XII)

Since the end of the 1960s, UK-flagged pleasure craft over 13.7m (approximately 45ft) have also been obliged to comply with the Merchant Shipping (Life-Saving Appliances for Ships other than Ships of Classes III to VI (A)) Regulations 1999 and the Merchant Shipping (Fire Protection: Small Craft) Regulations 1998.

In May 2002, the owner of a privately-owned 15m motor cruiser was prosecuted by The Maritime and Coastguard Agency (MCA) – after the vessel ran aground on a breakwater – for not keeping a proper look out (a breach of the Colregs) and for having out-of-date flares, lifebuoys which were in a poor state of repair and without lights and no smoke floats. In short, the vessel did not meet the requirements of the Regulations and the owner was fined a total of £2500 with costs of £3500 awarded to the MCA.

Appreciating that technology had moved on, the British Maritime Federation (BMF) and the RYA agreed with the MCA an 'Exemption' that allowed equipment designed for private boats to be used while still meeting the requirements of the Regulations. Owners therefore can choose to either comply in full with either the Merchant Shipping Regulations or ensure their boat meets the equivalent standards listed in the Exemption.

The equipment required in the Exemption is shown in the following tables. For life saving appliances and summoning help, the equipment required varies depending on the distance from the coast that the vessel will be operating (see Table 1). For fire fighting, the equipment required depends on the displacement and length of the vessel (see Table 2).

Table 1 – Life saving appliances required on craft over 13.7m but less than 24m in length

Items	Distance voyaging off coast			
	Less than 3 miles	3 to 20 miles	20 to 150 miles	Over 150 miles
Lifebuoys, line thrower and buoyant lines	Two lifebuoys, one of which is fitted with a self-igniting light and a buoyant lifeline at least 18m in length.			Four lifebuoys, two of which are fitted with buoyant lifelines and two with self-igniting lights and self-activating smoke signals and a line-throwing appliance.
Lifejackets	A lifejacket suitable for a person weighing 32 kilogrammes or more for each such person on board; a lifejacket suitable for a person weighing less than 32 kilogrammes for each such person on board. Lifejackets carried for persons on watch should be stowed in positions readily accessible from the manned watch station.			
Lifejacket lights	No requirement.	Each lifejacket shall be fitted with a lifejacket light complying with the appropriate MCA recognised standard.		
Flares	4 red hand-held, 4 white hand-held and 2 orange smoke flares	4 parachute flares, 4 red hand-held, 4 white hand-held and 2 orange smoke flares		
Training/instruction manual	A training or instruction manual containing instructions and information on the life-saving appliances provided in the vessel and their maintenance.			
Lifesaving signals	A copy of the table "Life-saving Signals and Rescue Methods, SOLAS No. 1" or "Life-saving Signals and Rescue Methods, SOLAS No. 2".			
Maritime radio	A maritime radio capable of transmitting and receiving, appropriate to the area of operation.			
Boarding ladder	In ships of Class XII of 13.7m in length and over, an embarkation ladder shall be provided at each embarkation station extending, in a single length, from the deck to the waterline in the lightest seagoing condition under unfavourable conditions of trim of up to 10 degrees and with the ship listed not less than 20 degrees either way and where such distance exceeds 1 metre. Such ladder(s) may be temporarily attached. In ships of Class XII of 13.7m in length or over, but less than 24m in length, such ladder(s) may be replaced by approved devices to afford access to survival craft when waterborne.			
One or more inflatable liferaft(s) with total capacity to accommodate those on board	No requirement	Yes[1]	Yes[2]	Yes[3]

Notes:

[1] = The liferaft(s) provided should be either:-

- SOLAS standard, Wheelmarked or DTLR (Dept. of Transport, Local Government and the Regions) approved, except that the liferaft(s) should be equipped with SOLAS B pack ; or

- International Sailing Federation (ISAF), Offshore Special Regulations (OSR) Appendix A Part 2. Equipped to a level equivalent to that of a "SOLAS B pack". This may, where necessary, include a 'grab bag' to supplement the equipment in the liferaft; or

- International Sailing Federation (ISAF), Offshore Special Regulations (OSR) Appendix A Part 1 requirements and manufactured prior to 1st July 2003, until replacement is due or the end date of this exemption (12th September 2012) whichever date occurs first. Liferaft(s) should be equipped to a level equivalent to that of a SOLAS B pack. This may, where necessary, include a 'grab bag' to supplement the equipment in the liferaft; or

- ISO 9650-1:2005 – Small Craft Inflatable Liferafts Part 1 Type 1 Group A standard provided the liferaft(s) are fitted with a boarding ramp; and are equipped to the level of a SOLAS B pack. This may, where necessary, include a 'grab bag' to supplement the equipment in the liferaft; or

- ISO 9650-2:2005 – Small Craft Liferafts Part 2 Type 2 ; or

- an equivalent capacity CE marked Category C rigid or inflated inflatable dinghy ready for immediate use.

[2] = as 1 but excluding the last two options (ISO 9650-2:2005 – Small Craft Liferafts Part 2 Type 2 or an equivalent capacity CE marked Category C rigid or inflated inflatable dinghy ready for immediate use)

[3] = The liferaft(s) provided should be constructed to SOLAS standard, Wheelmarked or DTLR approved, except that the liferaft(s) should be equipped with a SOLAS A pack.

Table 2 – Fire fighting appliances required on craft over 13.7m and under 24m

	Every ship of 13.7 metres in length or over, but less than 24 metres in length, shall be provided with:
Fire extinguisher	Not less than four multi-purpose fire extinguishers to a recognised standard, each with a minimum fire rating of 13A/113B, or a combination of smaller extinguishers giving the equivalent fire rating; or (a) Not less than two multi-purpose fire extinguishers as described above, and (b) A fire pump capable of delivering one jet of water with a minimum throw of 6 metres with a 6mm nozzle to any part of the ship. The fire pump, which need not be a dedicated fire pump, shall have one fire hose of adequate length with a 6mm nozzle and a suitable spray nozzle, and shall be either: (i) a hand powered fire pump, fixed or portable, outside any engine space with one sea and hose connections; or (ii) a power driven fire pump outside any engine space, fixed or portable, with sea and hose connections; or (iii) a hand powered portable fire pump with a throw over sea suction and hose connection. *Note: Multi-purpose fire extinguishers shall have a capability to deal with both Category A fires involving solid materials, and Category B fires, involving liquids or liquefiable solids. Portable fire extinguishers provided in compliance with these Regulations shall be of approved types and /or technically equivalent to BS EN3.*
Fire buckets	Not less than two fire buckets with lanyards. Fire buckets may be of metal, plastic or canvas and should be suitable for their intended service.

Boats used on inland waterways – The Boat Safety Scheme

Boats used on the UK's inland waterways are subject to the standards set in The Boat Safety Scheme. British Waterways and the Environment Agency set up the Scheme to minimise the risks of fires or explosions on boats by specifying a set of requirements that most boats must meet before they can be granted a navigation licence. The Scheme also recommends a number of 'safety best practice' measures to enhance the safety and personal health of those on board.

Boats have to be inspected once every four years by a registered Boat Safety Scheme examiner.

It applies to all boats based on British Waterways managed navigations and most Environment Agency waters. It is endorsed by all UK navigation authorities represented by the Association of Inland Navigation Authorities and is a requirement of the Broads Authority. Some navigation authorities may allow a short term or visitor status licence without the need to undergo a BSS examination if the owner makes a declaration that their boat meets the authority's legal requirements outlined in the BSS guide.

Some Authorities accept craft under 4 years old that conform to the RCD and meet their requirements. For further information see www.boatsafetyscheme.com.

Manning

Exemptions to the Merchant Shipping (Safe Manning, Hours of Work and Watchkeeping) Regulations 1997 have been granted to pleasure vessels of less than 3000grt. For vessels of or exceeding 24m load line length and 80grt or more, MSN1802 details the manning requirements and MGN 156 the deck and engineering requirements. Craft of less than 24m (load line) length or less than 80grt simply need not comply. Therefore if your vessel is not used for financial gain and is either less than 24m (load line) length or less than 80grt, there is no requirement for you to have a certificate of competence to skipper the vessel in UK territorial waters or on the high seas.

Boating abroad – International Certificate of Competence

If sailing overseas, some countries require evidence of the skipper's competence to operate a boat.

The United Nations Economic Commission for Europe Inland Transport Committee Resolution 40 International Certificate for Operators of Pleasure Craft – known in the UK as the International Certificate of Competence (ICC) – often provides the appropriate assurance. While only a few countries have signed up to the Resolution, many more countries are content with the ICC as evidence of competence.

Broadly speaking, an ICC is required for the inland waterways of Europe and for inland and coastal waters of Mediterranean countries. It is not usually required in the coastal waters of Northern Europe but there are exceptions.

The RYA is the UK's issuing authority for the ICC. To obtain an ICC you must prove your competence. An RYA practical course may be sufficient, if not then you will need to take a practical test at a recognised training establishment. The UK (RYA) ICC has six categories – Coastal, Inland, Sail, Power up to 10m, Power 10m and over and Personal Watercraft. Only the categories for which competence has been proven can be validated. The Code Européen des Voies de la Navigation Intérieure, better known as CEVNI, governs navigation on many of Europe's waterways – the equivalent of the sea-going COLREGs. European inland waterways have specific rules and use different signage for navigation. A test on these rules must be passed before an ICC valid for inland waters can be issued.

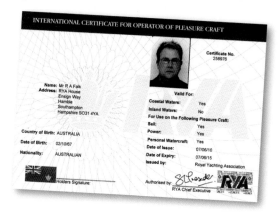

See 'Boating Abroad' on the RYA website for more detailed advice.

Sailing yacht racing – ISAF regulations

The International Sailing Federation owns the Racing Rules of Sailing and special regulations for offshore races but individual classes (from dinghies as small as Optimists to offshore yachts as large as 60ft multihulls) often make their own rules. The organisation also gives clear requirements on the type and condition of safety equipment that has to be carried when racing. The RYA publication YR9 Racing Yacht Safety has further details. Also visit the ISAF website and, for sailing yachts in particular, the 'Offshore Special Regulations' section of the website.

Regulations for commercial craft – Small Commercial Vessel and Pilot Boat (SCV) Code

Leisure boat owners need to be aware that should they use their craft at sea other than as a pleasure vessel – for example for commercial, chartering or sea school training – they are required to ensure their boats meet the standards of construction, stability, safety and fit out of the MCA's Small Commercial Vessel and Pilot Boat (SCV) Code as shown in MGN280 (M). Details of the standard can be found on the RYA's website.

The RYA's technical department can provide further advice and, as an MCA

Certifying Authority, can undertake the required water condition survey and stability assessment, and check the safety equipment meets the required standard.

Reporting Accidents

In the UK, unless you are chartering a boat, there is no legislation that requires pleasure boat owners, skippers or crew to report any major incidents.

In a correction to the Marine Guidance Note number 289 issued by the MCA in 2005 to announce the introduction of The Merchant Shipping (Accident Reporting and Investigation) Regulations 2005, pleasure boats are exempted from the requirements to report accidents unless they are recreational craft hired on a bareboat basis. And in their case it is only for certain types of accident – i.e. ones that lead to explosion, fire, death, major injury, capsize of a power-driven craft or boat or pollution causing significant harm to the environment. It's worth noting that the regulations apply to all UK vessels wherever they might be and to any vessel which is in the UK or UK waters.

Explosion, fire, death, capsize and pollution are self evident. Major injury includes any fracture to or loss of a major limb, loss of sight or other injury requiring resuscitation or leading to hypothermia or admittance to a hospital or other medical facility for more than 24 hours.

If any of those misfortunes should happen to you when chartering then you are required to report the accident to the Marine Accident Investigation Branch – see page 156. The MAIB's role is to investigate why and how the accident happened, rather than to lay blame with the aim to prevent similar accidents.

Accidents must be reported by the quickest means possible so that they can be investigated before evidence is lost or removed. They can be reported on line via the MAIB website or by a dedicated 24-hour accident phone line +44 (0) 23 8023 2527.

Obviously, any accident in UK waters that leads to death on any vessel will also need to be investigated by the police to ensure foul play has not taken place.

Recreational Craft Directive

Made mandatory on 16 June 1998, the European Recreational Craft Directive sets out minimum standards for construction, buoyancy and stability and limited requirements for safety features and equipment for recreational craft from 2.5 to 24 metres. It applies to vessels sold, placed on the market or brought into use, in countries belonging to the European Community.

Basically, the RCD is designed to provide a single specification that removes any previous barriers to trade created by each country having its own requirements. Its benefit to providing good levels of safety is limited. Just because a boat is specified to meet the standard doesn't mean to say that it is ready to go to sea.

The Directive is not enforced on craft built, or brought in to service, before 16 June 1998.

To set the standards, vessels are categorised as to their suitability for use in one (occasionally two) of four categories which outline the area of operation and the weather and sea conditions they are expected to withstand.

The RCD also puts other requirements on the vessel such as engine noise and engine exhaust emission limits, electromagnetic interference limits, the CE marking etc. But from the point of view of safety, it's the stability and construction elements of the categories that provide a guide to a boat's suitability for purpose. It should also ensure that at least a limited amount of safety equipment is provided with a (new) boat.

Category A: Ocean

Boats designed for extended voyages where conditions may exceed Force 8 wind and significant wave heights of 4m and above but excluding abnormal conditions. Vessels are largely self sufficient. Boats in this category are likely to be larger than 10m LOA.

Category B: Offshore

Boats designed for offshore voyages where conditions up to and including Force 8 wind and significant wave heights up to and including 4m may be experienced. Boats in this category are likely to be between 8m and 13.7m.

Category C: Inshore

Boats designed for voyages in coastal waters, large bays, estuaries, lakes and rivers where conditions up to and including Force 6 wind and significant wave heights up to and including 2m may be experienced. Boats in this category are likely to be less than 8m LOA.

Category D: Sheltered Waters

Boats designed for voyages on sheltered coastal waters, small bays, small lakes, rivers and canals where conditions up to and including Force 4 winds and significant wave heights up and including 0.3m may be experienced with occasional waves of 0.5m maximum height from, for example, passing vessels. Boats in this category are likely to be less than 6m LOA.

Be aware that significant wave height refers to the average height of the third of the highest waves. It is entirely possible that waves of double this height may be experienced.

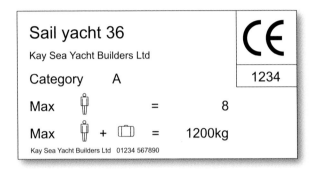

To show that a boat conforms to the RCD, a Builder's Plate is fitted to the boat. It must show the vessel's RCD category, the maximum number of people and the maximum load (including people) in Kg that the boat can carry. On larger vessels, the plate can cause confusion. For example, it may indicate as many as 20 people can be carried, however, this could contradict the Merchant Shipping Regulations limit of no more than 12 passengers depending on how many people on board are not directly involved in the running of the vessel.

In the UK, there are no laws that require recreational boats to operate within prescribed limits. However, some European countries have been known to prosecute owners who use their boats in conditions outside of the vessel's RCD category.

Chapter 3 Lifejackets and Buoyancy Aids

The RYA recommends that a lifejacket (or buoyancy aid) should be worn at all times when afloat unless it's safe to take it off.

Lifejacket or buoyancy aid?

New lifejackets sold in Europe must have a CE mark and meet the international standard ISO 12402, although those manufactured to the European standard EN 396 that have not had a design change can still be made and sold. Where the new standard is making significant differences is to the quality of construction and materials used in the manufacture of the PFD (Personal Flotation Device). Note that lifejackets made to the United States requirements – which are sometimes imported with American boats – do not meet the ISO standard and may not provide as much buoyancy.

The ISO standard has not yet been fully implemented throughout Europe and continues to develop with, for example, more work being undertaken on the fitting of crotch straps to inflatable lifejackets. It's the development of several years of PFD design and builds not only on the EN standard but on the British Standard before that.

The standard set the minimum levels of buoyancy required for each type of jacket, however, there are now several PFDs on the market that exceed the required level. For example, it's not unusual to find lifejackets that meet the Level 150 standard but provide 175N of buoyancy.

You will need to choose a PFD that is appropriate to the activity.

As a general guideline, buoyancy aids are suitable for use on those occasions when you expect to go into the water and need to be able to swim easily:

- Personal watercraft
- Water skiing
- Sailing dinghies
- Windsurfers
- Providing safety cover for such activities

Lifejackets are suitable for use on:

- An open boat such as a powerboat or RIB
- The boat's tender
- A sailing yacht or motor cruiser
- Or any other occasion when you are not expecting to go into the water.

In an ideal world, it's better not to go into the water when you are not wanting to!

The current ISO standards give buoyancy ratings in Newtons (N)

ISO 12402-5 / EN 393 – Level 50 buoyancy aid (50N)

ISO 12402-4 / EN 395 – Level 100 lifejacket (100N)

ISO 12402-3 / EN396 – Level 150 lifejacket (150N)

ISO 12402-2 / EN 399 – Level 275 lifejacket (275N)

Children's lifejackets have equivalent buoyancy ratings as adults' lifejackets – e.g. 50N and 150N – but with reduced buoyancy to suit their smaller size. Most have crotch straps to help prevent the buoyancy aid from riding up in the water. Some also include a harness so that the child can be tethered to the boat and prevented from falling in the first place. It's essential that children wear the correct size lifejacket or buoyancy aid. Don't buy one they will grow into!

Level 50 buoyancy aids are designed for competent swimmers as an aid to flotation in inshore waters where help is close at hand. They are suitable for those who expect to go in the water – dinghy sailors, waterskiers, kayakers etc – allowing them to swim easily back to their craft. They are comfortable to wear and provide a modicum of padded protection, with usually one or several layers of closed cell foam, should the wearer fall in the boat. They provide buoyancy without impeding the movement of the wearer. They are not designed to turn the wearer face up.

Sold in several sizes from child to XXL, buoyancy aids need to be a snug fit to work properly. To check the size, don the buoyancy aid and try lifting the jacket at the shoulders. If it lifts more than 50mm (two inches) it's too big.

Level 100 lifejackets are designed to keep non-swimmers afloat but not necessarily turn an unconscious wearer face up. Like buoyancy aids, they are usually made from one or several layers of closed-cell foam and sold in several sizes from child to XXL. The correct size must be worn for the lifejacket to work properly. Check for size by lifting jacket at shoulders. If it lifts more than 50mm (two inches) it's too big.

Level 150 lifejackets are the standard lifejackets suitable for swimmers and non-swimmers and arguably the best type for offshore boats. Although designed to turn an unconscious wearer face up, air trapped in waterproof clothing may not allow the jacket to right the person immediately.

The lifejacket will give a reasonable chance of survival but will hamper movement when fully deployed. Most jackets of this size are gas-inflated, however, bulky all foam or foam and air jackets are also available.

Level 275 lifejackets were designed to provide sufficient buoyancy to self-right an offshore oil worker wearing an immersion suit. It's a high performance lifejacket, suitable for severe offshore conditions and for those carrying significant weights such as tools.

Usually gas inflated and consisting of one or, sometimes, two separate bladders, its extra buoyancy is designed to counteract trapped air in waterproof clothing. Unfortunately, its large deployed size can make it difficult for the wearer to climb into a liferaft or up a boarding ladder.

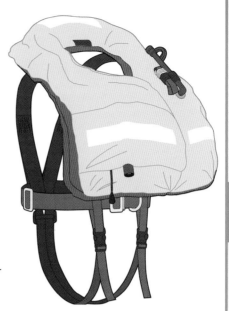

Gas lifejacket

Gas lifejackets are inflated with carbon dioxide (CO_2) stored under pressure in a sealed metal cylinder. The gas is released by piercing the seal either manually by pulling the toggle or automatically on immersion if fitted with an automatic firing head.

It is essential to fit the correct size cylinder for the size of lifejacket. Too big a cylinder may burst the jacket, too small a cylinder will not fully inflate the bladder. The correct size cylinder will fully inflate the jacket in under five seconds.

The lifejacket has to be worn outside of clothing. If it inflates underneath a waterproof jacket, the wearer's chest will be squeezed making it impossible to draw breath. Make sure that the manual inflation toggle is always available – do not tuck it inside the jacket.

Types of inflation

Oral only inflation

It is possible to obtain oral-inflation lifejackets. These do not have a gas cylinder. They are inflated by blowing through an inflation tube. Because of the physiological effects of falling into water, it is unlikely that you will be able to inflate the lifejacket. They are not recommended for everyday use on a boat.

Manual gas inflation

The jacket is inflated by pulling on the toggle. It will not inflate automatically when the wearer goes into the water. The firing mechanism has some means of indicating if the jacket has been fired – often it is as simple as a small green clip over the toggle lever. Whether this is present or not, it is sensible to unscrew the cylinder and check the seal has not been pierced.

Automatic gas/cartridge inflation

There are several different designs of automatic gas inflation firing heads that give various degrees of protection to the cartridge or pill. They allow the jacket to be triggered either manually by pulling on the toggle (its primary method of firing) or automatically on immersion.

Automatic operation uses a spring-loaded plunger held in place either by a compacted paper cartridge or pill. When the cartridge or pill becomes wet it expands or dissolves, releasing the plunger so that it pushes the pin through the gas cylinder seal, releasing the gas into the lifejacket bladder.

In addition to a manual indicator, automatic firing mechanisms have a separate indicator to show they have not been operated. When donning the lifejacket check the automatic firing head and the manual indicators. If one or other is not present unscrew and check that the seal on the cylinder has not been pierced.

Although different makes of lifejackets may appear to have identical firing heads they are often not interchangeable.

Some automatic firing heads can fire accidentally if they become excessively wet.

Automatic heads have a limited life and will be marked either with an expiry date or a date of manufacture.

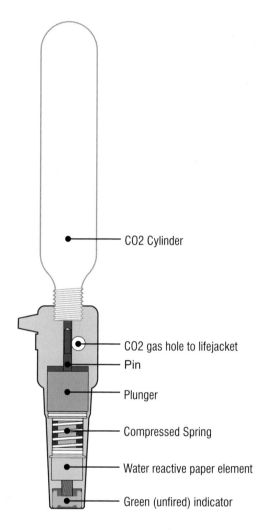

CO2 Cylinder

CO2 gas hole to lifejacket

Pin

Plunger

Compressed Spring

Water reactive paper element

Green (unfired) indicator

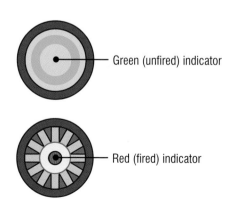

Green (unfired) indicator

Red (fired) indicator

Hammar automatic inflation

The Hammar system protects the water sensitive element with a hydrostatic valve that prevents accidental activation by wave splash, heavy rain or spray. The valve opens after two to three seconds immersion at a depth of 100mm (4 inches). This allows water to reach the water sensitive element, which dissolves and triggers the pin to pierce the cylinder.

When the jacket is fired manually, the toggle detaches from the firing head.

The firing head will show a green indicator if it has not been fired and a red one if it has. Hammar automatic inflation heads have a five-year life. The replacement date is printed on the firing head. Keep spare re-arming kits on board so that the jacket can be re-armed immediately.

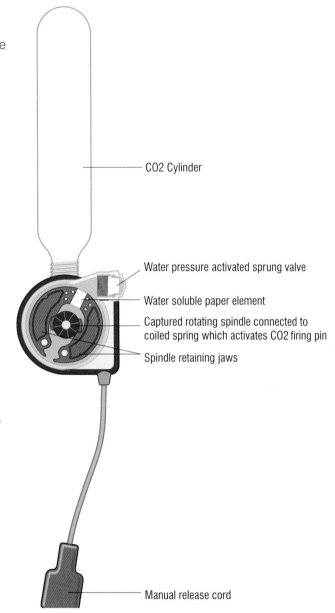

CO2 Cylinder

Water pressure activated sprung valve

Water soluble paper element

Captured rotating spindle connected to coiled spring which activates CO2 firing pin

Spindle retaining jaws

Manual release cord

Auto inflation lifejackets on helicopters
Automatic lifejackets are not to be worn on helicopters since if the aircraft should ditch the lifejacket would inflate inside the cabin and prevent the wearer from escaping. SAR helo crew will ask for the auto heads to be removed before winching a casualty aboard. Some lifejackets can be easily converted to manual operation.

Lifejacket standard fittings and extras

To meet the standard, a lifejacket will come as standard with a whistle, buddy strap, retro-reflective tape and, if a gas inflatable, with an oral inflation tube and a gas inflation system. Whether it's automatic or manual is up to you. But there are a number of optional extras that, depending on the type of boating, should be considered essential.

Crotch or thigh straps help to hold the lifejacket down and lift the wearer's airway higher out of the water. Without them, the wearer is likely to slip lower in the lifejacket. If and when he falls unconscious, due to the effects of hypothermia or because of a blow on the head, the wearer may well drown in the lifejacket. Crotch straps should be considered essential extras. If the lifejacket is not supplied with crotch straps, they can be bought separately and retrofitted to existing lifejackets.

Safety harness Gas inflated lifejackets are usually offered with the option of a built-in safety harness. The harness should be made to the harness standard of either ISO 12401 or EN1095. The harnesses are principally designed for if crew fall overboard,

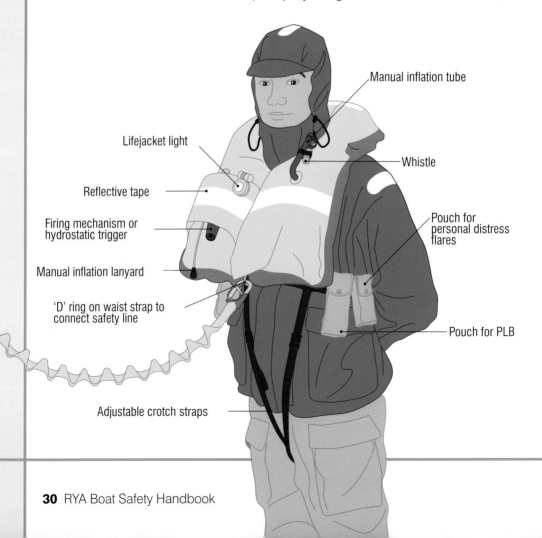

Manual inflation tube

Lifejacket light

Whistle

Reflective tape

Firing mechanism or hydrostatic trigger

Pouch for personal distress flares

Manual inflation lanyard

'D' ring on waist strap to connect safety line

Pouch for PLB

Adjustable crotch straps

with the safety harness attachment eye easily accessible to attach the safety lanyard and able to withstand the impact loads of a crew member falling overboard. However, the attachment point will be difficult, if not impossible, to access when the jacket is inflated.

Folded inside all inflatable jackets, whether they have a safety harness or not, there is a lifting loop. It becomes accessible when the jacket is inflated. The loop can be used to attach a lifting line to recover the MOB. It is not designed to take the impact loads of a safety harness.

The choice of a **built-in harness** that allows the wearer to fit a safety lanyard and clip on to strong points or jack stays on the vessel will depend on the type of boating – see MOB Prevention on page 38.

The adoption of further parts of ISO 12402 will introduce the requirement for **status indicators.** Some manufacturers are already offering them with some lifejackets. The firing head can be seen through a small clear window on the outside of the jacket and have indicators to show if the cylinder and, if fitted, the automatic cartridge or pill, is operational. Green indicates OK, red means replace. It is still advisable to regularly check the cylinder is securely screwed into the firing head.

Even though only planning to use your boat during daylight hours, consideration needs to be given to fitting a **lifejacket light.** In reality, most daylight boaters tend to return just before dusk. One needs to consider that if disaster struck on the return journey, how long would it take for the alarm to be raised and for help to reach the casualties. Will it be dark? In which case, you need a lifejacket light.

Liifejacket lights are available either as static, flashing or strobe lights. Some will function automatically on immersion. Better quality lights are built to SOLAS requirements and provide 0.75 candela for at least 8 hours.

Sprayhoods increase your chances of survival in wind and waves

When wearing a lifejacket in wind and waves, your feet act like a drogue and cause you to turn to face the spume and waves. A sprayhood assists by minimising the amount of spray and water that can reach the user's airway. This is particularly important for a casualty that is injured or beginning to tire while awaiting rescue.

A spray hood, either fitted into the collar of the lifejacket or held in a separate pouch on the waist belt, can be donned and will significantly reduce the effects of breaking waves. They also help to hold in heat and, because of their bright colour, make the wearer more visible from all angles.

Safety lanyards/buddy straps can be used to clip casualties together thereby preventing them from drifting apart and provide a bigger target for rescuers to see.

Personal locator beacons and MOB alarms – see page 44.

Personal pyrotechnics – day/night flares can be carried in a pouch attached to the lifejacket's waist belt. (see page 92)

Rearming packs

The damp atmosphere inside a closed cabin after a wet weekend's sailing can trigger some automatic gas-inflation systems to inflate the jacket. Very wet boating conditions may also cause a jacket to inflate inadvertently.

Spare rearming packs need to be carried on board so that the lifejacket can be re-armed and made operational immediately. A fired, deflated jacket is not a lifejacket.

Donning a gas-inflated lifejacket

For the lifejacket to work, it must be worn correctly. Too slack and the wearer may slip down or even out of the jacket when in the water or when being lifted back aboard the boat.

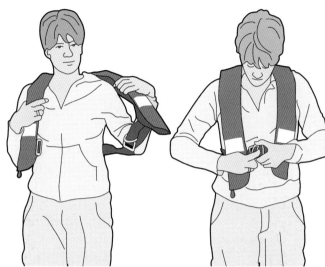

1. Put the jacket on like a waistcoat. Hold the jacket the right way up and put your right arm between the jacket front and the back strap.

2. Pull jacket across back and put left arm between left jacket front and back strap.

3. Fasten clip at front of jacket. Check it is secure.

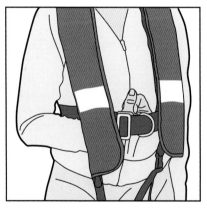

5. Adjust the waist belt so that it is a tight fit when your fist is placed between strap and chest. This will prevent the jacket from squeezing your chest when it inflates yet without it being too slack.

4.Reach down and pull the crotch strap or thigh straps between legs and clip to waist belt. Shorten the straps to take up slack but not so tight as to be uncomfortable.

> **Lifejacket design is improving but there are still many that require several minutes to adjust.**

Lifejacket maintenance and checks

Most manufacturers recommend that gas-inflated lifejackets should be professionally serviced annually or biannually. Under Class XII (see page 16), boats 13.7m and over are required to have their lifejackets serviced at the manufacturer's recommended interval by an approved agent.

A full service will include recorded pressure checks of the bladder and checks of the firing mechanism as well as washing, general maintenance and a detailed inspection.

Between service periods it's advisable to check and maintain the lifejacket regularly to ensure correct operation.

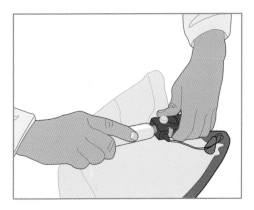

Regularly check that the gas cylinder is securely tightened into the firing mechanism. If it is loose, it may not fire and, because it is not seated correctly, the gas will escape and the jacket will not inflate fully.

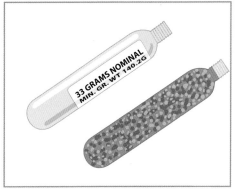

Inspect the gas cylinder for corrosion that can cause small pin holes in the lifejacket bladder. Check the cylinder is the correct size for the lifejacket.

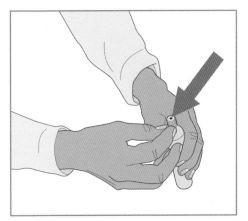

Unscrew the cylinder and check the seal is still secure. If it has a hole in it then fit replacement cylinder.

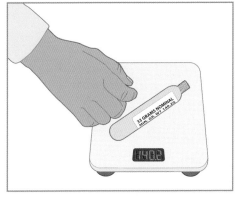

Weigh the cylinder on a digital scale to ensure it matches its gross weight embossed on the cylinder. A 33g cylinder has a gross weight around 140g.

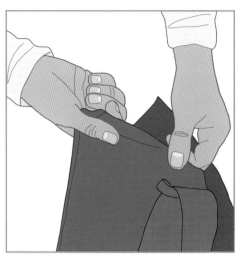

Unfold the lifejacket and inspect the cover and bladder for punctures, cracks, wear and tear.

> **TIP**
> Since not all manufacturers air test their lifejackets it's a good practice to inflate, preferably using an air pump through the oral tube, all lifejackets immediately after purchase to ensure the bladder does not leak.

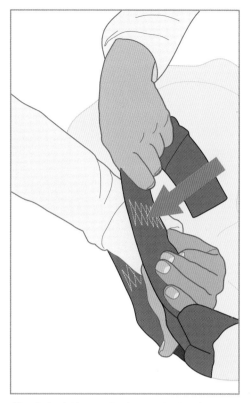

Check the belts are firmly attached to the lifejacket. Inspect stitching for wear.

Every three to six months

Remove the gas cylinder and inflate the jacket, preferably with an air pump, through the oral inflation tube. Leave the jacket inflated for 24 hours to check that it is airtight. When not being used regularly, unfold the jacket and store on a wooden clothes hanger.

To deflate, push in the valve in the oral inflation tube by using the cap on the tube. Do not use any other item to push into the tube since it may damage or dislodge the valve. Squeeze the jacket tightly to exhale the gas. Make sure all gas is removed before reattaching the gas cylinder and re-packing.

Rearming automatic lifejackets

On automatic lifejackets with cartridges, bobbins or pills, some manufacturers recommend removing the automatic cartridge before removing the gas cylinder to prevent damage to the firing head's piercing pin. Discard the old cylinder and automatic cartridge before fitting the new cylinder to prevent refitting a fired cylinder. Fitting a spent auto head will pierce and waste a new cylinder.

Looking after man's best friend

All dogs can swim but owners become understandably alarmed when their best friend goes overboard. The resulting panic can lead to other accidents and owners will often risk their own lives in a bid to save the animal.

A lifejacket gives the dog extra buoyancy and, perhaps best of all, a good attachment point with which to handle the dog between boats and to recover him after he's fallen in.

Check the lifejacket provides full support beneath the animal to avoid injury when lifting. As with buoyancy aids, getting the right size is essential.

A harness point on the lifejacket allows the animal to be clipped on to the boat to prevent a DOB in the first place.

Airlines and gas-inflated lifejackets

Compressed gas is normally classified as a dangerous good that passengers may not carry on board an aircraft. However, the Civil Aviation Authority has confirmed that, with the approval of the airline, up to two small (33g) carbon dioxide cylinders fitted into a gas-inflation lifejacket plus two spare cylinders and may be carried as part of a passenger's luggage.

Get written consent from the airline at the time of booking to take with you on the flight – otherwise the lifejackets may be confiscated.

Stowage

There should be a lifejacket for each person on board and at least one or more spares. Lifejackets should be stored hanging in a relatively dry environment. They should be rinsed in fresh water regularly and allowed to dry away from direct sunlight before stowing.

Why wear a lifejacket?

The waters around the British Isles are officially recognised as being part of a cold water region. It's coldest during February, when the sea temperature is likely to drop to around 4°C to 6°C and builds during the Spring and Summer to a maximum temperature in August of between 14°C to 18°C depending on whether you are in the North, South, East or West.

The colder the water, the stronger the effects on the human body. While many believe hypothermia is the main threat to life, in reality you are more likely to drown than die from cold.

There are four stages associated with sudden immersion – cold water shock, swim failure, hypothermia and post-rescue collapse. The first three stages are all likely to lead to drowning. Cold water shock occurs in the first three to five minutes of immersion. On entering cold water, the body responds with a rapid increase in heart rate. At rest, the heart beats at around 60 to 70 beats/minute. On immersion this increases to as much as 150 to 180 beats/minute, putting tremendous strain on the circulatory system, with the possibility of cardiac arrest or stroke.

Breathing also increases rapidly from an at-rest rate of around 12 breaths/minute to around 60 breaths/minute (one a second), increasing your breathing volume to 114lt/minute. The effect of the cold also makes it impossible to hold your breath, so you are highly likely to breathe in when under water.

The lethal aspiration limit for sea water is 22 millilitres/kg of the casualty's body weight. For the average adult that means you only need to aspirate about 1.5lt to drown. Even a small amount of the water in the lungs reduces their ability to transfer oxygen to the blood.

Most deaths in water occur within 3 metres of safety because of the effects of cold water shock. If you survive the first few minutes the next stage is swim failure. In this stage, which takes place between 5 to 30 minutes after immersion, the body tries to conserve heat by reducing blood flow to the limbs. Our muscles need oxygenated blood to work. Without it, it becomes impossible to co-ordinate our limbs for swimming. Consequently, the casualty without a lifejacket is unable to keep their airway high enough out of the water and succumbs. It is estimated that over half of casualties without lifejackets drown during these first two stages.

After 30 minutes, the cooling of the body's deep tissues brings the onset of hypothermia and the casualty moves from confusion to unconsciousness. As soon as they become unconscious, the casualty without a lifejacket drowns. However, if wearing a lifejacket, the unconscious casualty can keep their airway clear of the water and is likely to stay alive for several hours more and thereby increase chances of rescue.

The facts speak for themselves. Whether you are new to boating or an old hand, a lifejacket considerably increases your chances of survival.

Chapter 4
MOB Prevention and Recovery

While there's much discussion about lifejackets and survival in the sea, it's easy to forget that the best form of protection is not to fall overboard in the first place.

Guard wires around the deck need to be sufficiently high for crew to brace their legs against rather than so low as to become a tripping hazard. ISAF regulations specify minimum heights for racing sailing yachts. Stanchions need to be firmly attached and the wire uncoated so that any corrosion can be easily identified. Check the end of the safety wires can be either easily released or are fastened with cord that can be cut quickly to aid MOB recovery.

If carrying small children or dogs/cats on board, fit netting to the guard wires to prevent them from slipping under the wire.

Deck Safety Harnesses

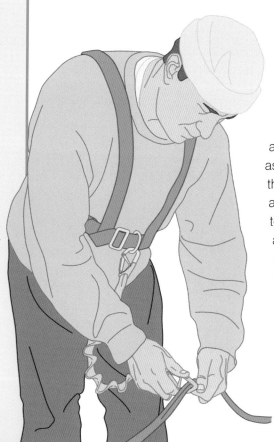

Most gas-inflated lifejackets are now available with integral harnesses and should be the preferred choice. However, harnesses can be bought and used separately. Whether the harness is part of a lifejacket or separate, it should meet the ISO 12401 (also known as EN1095) standard – which governs all aspects of the harness's construction from the strength of webbing to the stitching and attachment point. ISO 12401 also applies to safety lines and jack stays. Crotch straps are important to prevent the harness from slipping off when being used for lifting from the water.

Safety lines and jackstays

On sailing yachts, safety lines should be available for every member of the crew.

It's estimated that a 15 stone (100kg) man would exert a load of almost one tonne (2200lb) if falling over 6ft from deck to water, so the attachment points and fittings need to be strongly attached to the boat with appropriately sized backing pads. Standard safety lines tend to be 1.8m long but consideration should be given to shorter lines to prevent crew from falling longer distances. Harnesses are not designed to provide protection from a fall from height. Alternatively, when fitting jackstays, place them as close as possible to the centre of the boat to help prevent crew members from falling over the side, or halve the length of the line by threading it round the jackstay and clipping both hooks onto the harness D-ring.

Eyes for clipping on to should be positioned close to the cabin's companionway so that crew can clip on before exiting the cabin.

Safety tethers must have hooks at both ends so that crew can unhook themselves at their chest if need be. Three hook safety tethers allow crew to clip on to the next strong point before unclipping and provide a short tether option for working on the foredeck or at the mast.

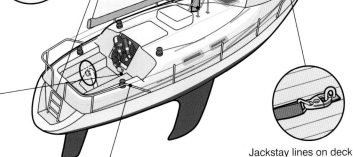

Granny bars around base of mast provide security for crew hoisting sails

Clip on before leaving cabin

Jackstay lines on deck

Guardwire pushpit lifelines attached by cord that can be cut or released quickly

Some safety lines are elasticated to take up slack when being used and reduce the chances of the line becoming snagged. Many include built-in stress indicators that show if the line has been overloaded and weakened. Overloaded line must be replaced.

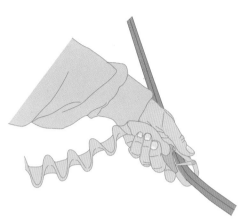

Hooks should be double action locking snap hooks such as the Gibb hook or Wichard hook. Carbine 'snap' hooks can roll out or capsize when turned around one leg of an u-shaped bolt.

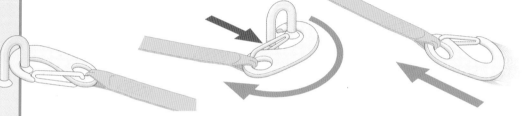

Jackstays can be made from polyester webbing or stainless steel wire. Webbing jackstays are degraded by sunlight – check and replace regularly. Wire jackstays can roll underfoot.

Fast boats

Do not clip on to planing or semi-displacement boats travelling at speed since being dragged alongside can cause severe injury. It's better to fall clear. However, if the boat is stopped or is moving at under 7 knots then clip on when going on deck i.e. when going forward to drop anchor in heavy weather. Though seldom seen on leisure motor craft, motorboats have jackstays fitted to provide secure anchor points to clip on to.

Never clip on to a fast motorboat when it's moving at speed

Man overboard flotation and position marking

Horsehoe lifebuoys are designed to provide easily deployed buoyancy for a person in the water. However, their light weight means they can be blown by the wind across the surface of the water faster than the MOB can swim after them. To slow the rate of drift fit the lifebuoy with a self-deploying drogue.

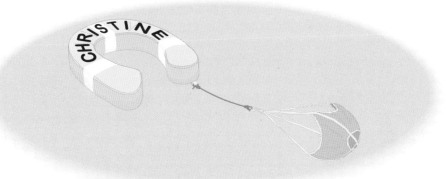

As with all buoyant equipment on board a boat, the lifebuoy should be marked with the boat's name or call sign. If picked up at sea, the SAR services have computer systems that can quickly track back where the lifebuoy came from taking into account the wind and tide conditions. If looking for survivors from a known vessel, finding a named lifebuoy may effect a change in their search patterns and increase the chances of rescue.

Check the lifebuoy is large enough and sufficiently flexible to be used – some lifebuoys are very brittle and can snap in the middle.

Automatic gas-inflated lifebuoys are also available. They use similar gas inflation systems to those fitted to gas-inflated lifejackets and inflate after they've entered the water. Consequently, they can be thrown greater distances and may land closer to the casualty.

Fitting retro-reflective tape around the lifebuoy in two or three places makes it significantly more visible in the light of a spotlight or torch.

Adding a floating line to the lifebuoy allows it to be retrieved after being thrown from a vessel.

Retro-reflective tape saves MOB

A SAR helicopter was searching for a man overboard (MOB) at dusk. The helicopter's thermal imaging camera was searching the area forward of the aircraft but without success. Daylight was going fast. The winch man, using the craft's searchlight from the starboard door, spotted a small glint of light in the distance. "Skipper, there's something in the distance at our three o'clock," he informed the pilot. "OK, we're not having much luck here, let's take a look," the pilot replied, turning the craft to port. As they closed on the target, the reflection grew brighter until they were hovering over the lost MOB, clinging to a horseshoe lifebuoy with retro-reflecting tape.
When the reflection was initially picked up, the helicopter was eight miles from the casualty.

True story recounted to the author by the SAR helo pilot.

Lifebuoy light

At least one lifebuoy on board should be fitted with an automatic light. Sadly, low cost models are notoriously unreliable, due to corrosion of the electrical contacts, and need to be checked before every night trip. Add name and retro-reflective tape.

Better quality lights, with integral 5-year life lithium batteries, meet the commercial standard set by the 1996-amended SOLAS 1974 code for life saving appliances. The lights are required to be white, provide a brightness of at least 2 candela and to provide either a steady light or a light flashing at a rate of approximately 60 flashes per minute.

Dan buoy

A dan buoy provides increased visibility of an MOB in waves. In addition to a flag – often signal flag Oscar meaning man overboard – some are fitted with an automatic light at the top of the pole. While often carried on sailing yachts, they are seldom found on motor cruisers because of the space required to stow them. Inflatable dan buoys take up much less space and are easier to deploy.

Avoid mounting a dan buoy on the port quarter of the cockpit – this is the area where a SAR helicopter crew will want to land.

The flag on a dan buoy should be flaked rather than rolled around the pole, to allow it to open easily after deployment.

A clip or small cover holds the flaked flag in place. Some dan buoys fly the signal flag O. Dan buoys should be attached to a lifering with a small drogue to minimise drift.

In daylight, a quickly deployed buoyant smoke flare not only helps mark the MOB's position, giving at least 3 minutes of smoke, but also raises the alarm to other boats within the vicinity. Stow the smoke flare in an easily accessible position close to the companionway. Short-handed crews in particular can easily lose sight of a MOB.

Whether sailing short-handed on a yacht or motor cruiser or aboard a multi-crew trans-ocean racing yacht, an MOB alarm can provide an immediate alert if somebody falls over the side. Broadly, these can be divided into two types – those that are based on 406/121.5MHz personal locator beacons (PLB) – which are described in more detail on page 88 – and those that comprise of a base station and a number of pendants or tags that are worn by the crew.

For the 406/121.5MHz PLB to sound an alarm on board the vessel, a 121.5MHz base station will need to be fitted. The station usually also includes a radio direction finder that allows those remaining on board to home in on to the MOB. Remember, that when a 406MHz beacon is operated it will also send an alert to the SAR authorities and the vessel will also need to contact the authorities to advise them of the actions being taken and whether any attempt at 'self-rescue' has been successful or not.

The proprietary systems that may be purchased may work in a different way. Some systems trigger a base station aboard the boat by sending a signal when the tag is immersed in the water, others use a proximity sensor – i.e. when the sensor goes beyond a certain range – usually about 10 to 20 metres – the base station detects its absence and sounds the alarm.

Some systems have a built-in GPS receiver that records the position when the alarm was triggered and provide a bearing and distance back to that position.

Others include a radio direction finder, tuned to the sensor's radio frequency, which provides a relative bearing to the MOB's transmitting sensor. The range of these beacons is usually up to 1 to 2 miles from the boat, depending on the height of the RDF's antenna – the sensor's antenna, of course, being at sea level. Much greater ranges are possible by SAR aircraft when using 121.5MHz, due to their height above the water.

The latest addition to MOB alerting systems is the AIS Personal Locator Beacon, which can be picked up by any vessel within range fitted with an AIS receiver – see page 84. If using the SAR homing frequency of 121.5MHz, SAR aircraft and lifeboats can also home in on the signal. In that case, it is essential to inform the SAR authorities that the casualty is wearing a 121.5MHz transmitter.

Alarm sounds when MOB is 10 metres from boat

10 metres

MOB

Man overboard recovery equipment

A boarding ladder on the transom of the boat may be ideal for a swimmer to climb back on board in calm water but it is not a safe place to recover a MOB in waves – the stern of a pitching boat can easily hit the MOB on the head or force them under the water.

With the exception of small boats such as dinghies and small sports boats, the best place to recover a MOB in waves is about half way along the length of the boat, where the boat moves least.

To recover the MOB here, even on a boat with low freeboard, will require some extra equipment. There's no one right way to recover a MOB. It will depend on your boat, how it is rigged and the state of the person in the water – for example; whether they are hypothermic, conscious or unconscious.

There are several methods. Some will require extra equipment, others will need no more than simply adapting what you already have on board.

Whichever method you decide will work best on your boat, it is essential that all the crew practise it at regular intervals and know how to rig the MOB recovery equipment.

To make the recovery easier, the lower guard wire around the boat should be able to be lowered. The connection between the lower guard wire and the pushpit may be either loops of cord, which can be cut, or a pelican hook. Pelican hooks can sometimes jam or, worse still, open without warning. Connections that cannot be released quickly should not be fitted.

Throwing lines and rescue strops

A purpose made (floating) throwing line allows the crew to get a line to the MOB quickly. A simple line can consist of no more than a ring and floating rope. More sophisticated options come in throw bags that unravel the rope when the bag is thrown. Ideally, the line needs to be at least 30m in length. Be aware that rope used for mooring warps sink and are not suitable for MOB throwing lines.

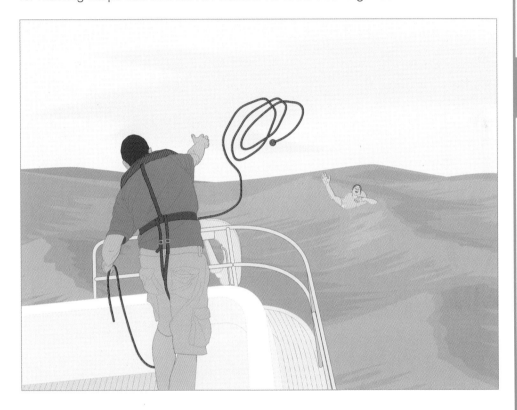

Getting a line around a MOB can be very difficult. If they are conscious, they may be able to don a boat rescue strop – a lighter-weight version of those seen on SAR helicopters. If not, then it may be necessary to lasso the MOB using a similar method to that of lassoing a mooring buoy. It will be painful for the MOB when he's lifted out of the water but better that than the consequences of remaining in the water.

If the MOB is wearing a lifejacket with a safety harness, a safety lanyard can be used to clip to the harness and attached to a lifting mechanism such as a halyard or handybilly (block and tackle). Be aware, that if the MOB is unconscious, it can be almost impossible to get close enough to attach a safety lanyard. Do not go into the water to assist. Use a dinghy or liferaft to get closer to the MOB.

Ladders and scramble nets

One simple solution is to fit a webbing safety ladder, held in a bag fastened to the toe rail or the bottom of a stanchion, at amidships. Only suitable for able-bodied crew, the ladder can be equipped with a short lanyard that allows it to be pulled out and down from the water.

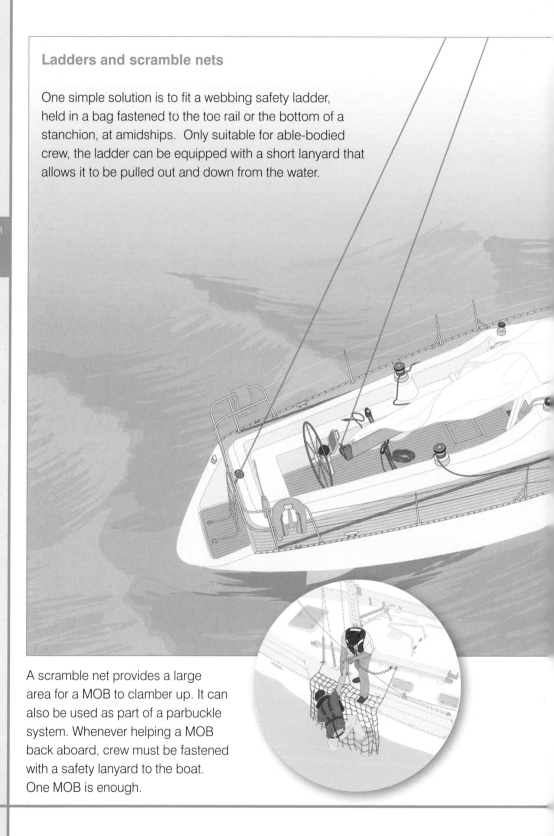

A scramble net provides a large area for a MOB to clamber up. It can also be used as part of a parbuckle system. Whenever helping a MOB back aboard, crew must be fastened with a safety lanyard to the boat. One MOB is enough.

TIP Many boats are fitted with fold-down boarding ladders on their transoms or bathing platforms. Fix a lanyard to the bottom rung of the ladder, just long enough to reach the water, so that anybody in the water can pull the ladder down. To prevent the ladder from toppling in when sailing, hold it in place with a pipe clip, rotten cotton or a pull-release knot such as slip clove hitch or highwayman's hitch.

Although not suitable for use in waves, if you fall out of your dinghy when going to the boat in the calm waters of an anchorage or mooring, it may well save your life.

Elevator method

The elevator method provides a quick way of helping a conscious MOB out of the water. All you need are two warps, a snatch block and a winch or windlass.

■ One warp is attached to a forward or midships cleat and led aft outside of the guard wires and either fed through the headsail traveller block, or led further aft through a snatch block, and back to the sheet winch.

■ The MOB stands on the bight of rope as it is winched tight, thereby lifting the MOB up the side of the boat. A second warp is rigged over the side of the boat as a manrope for the MOB to hold on to so that they don't fall backwards.

■ The MOB needs to shuffle their feet along the rope to avoid their legs being pulled sideways from beneath them.

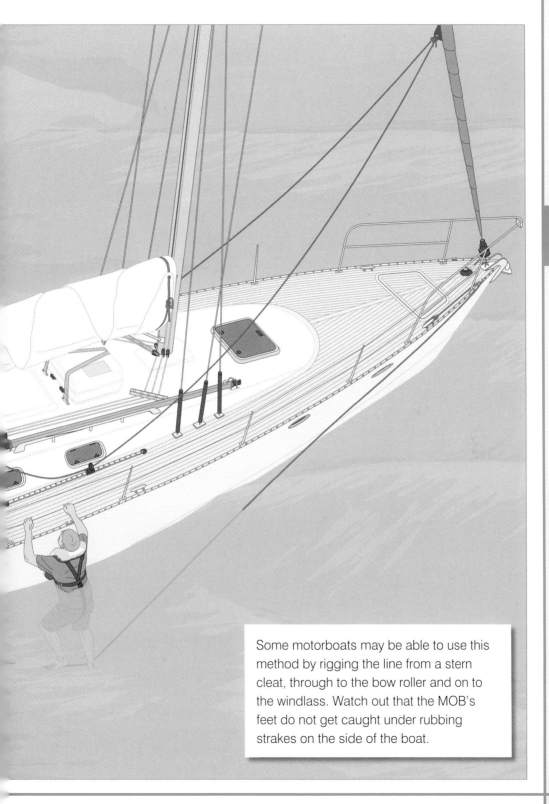

4

Some motorboats may be able to use this method by rigging the line from a stern cleat, through to the bow roller and on to the windlass. Watch out that the MOB's feet do not get caught under rubbing strakes on the side of the boat.

Boom lift

On yachts with booms fitted with kickers that can be released easily, it may be possible to use the boom as a derrick. The yacht needs to be sufficiently large to withstand lifting a MOB on the boom. A trailer-sailer is unlikely to have the stability or sufficiently strong rigging to use this method.

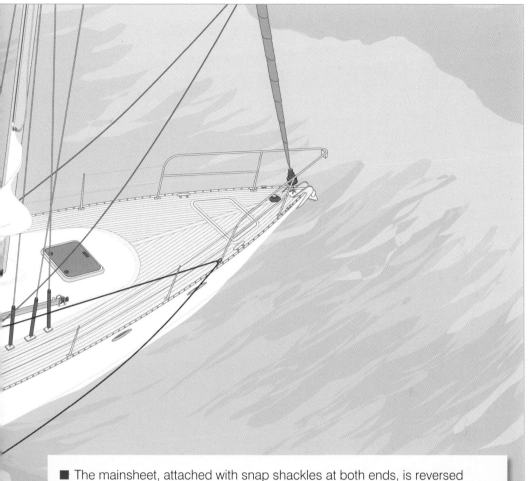

- The mainsheet, attached with snap shackles at both ends, is reversed and freed from the deck fitting. Attach preventers to stop the boom from swinging uncontrollably.

- Slacken off or unfasten the kicker, scandalise the boom to an angle of about 30 degrees above horizontal. It may be necessary to reinforce the topping lift with the halyard.

- Attach the bottom of the sheet either to the MOB's lifejacket or harness or to a rescue strop placed around the MOB's chest.

- Heave on the mainsheet or run the bitter end of the sheet to the sheet winch and lift the MOB into the yacht.

For hypothermic casualties, a horizontal lift can be achieved by placing an additional safety lanyard or line behind the knees of the MOB.

CHAPTER

4

RYA Boat Safety Handbook **53**

Parbuckle systems

A number of suppliers provide sheets or webbing nets that can be used to parbuckle the MOB back on board. Most are made by sail makers and consist of an isosceles triangle of strong gauze-like material with sturdy attachment points at each corner. It's important that they are made to an appropriate size to suit your boat's freeboard.

- The foot is fastened along the gunwale and the head is attached either to a halyard alone or to a handybilly (4:1 block and tackle) that is attached to a halyard.
- Lower the sheet into the water and position the MOB over the sheet.
- Heave on the halyard or handybilly.
- The bitter end of the handybilly can be led back to a sheet winch to provide greater mechanical advantage.
- The casualty will roll inside the parbuckle sheet, up and on to the sidedeck. The greatest difficulty in using this method is getting the MOB positioned into the sheet, especially when recovering in rough water.

A small headsail can be used in place of a purpose-designed parbuckle but it is not as good. It will be more difficult to get the sail to sink sufficiently to position the MOB in it. Also there's a strong possibility, because the luff and leach are different lengths that the MOB will slip out of the sail as he is being brought aboard.

MOB recovery raft

Inflatable one-man MOB recovery rafts, such as the Jonbuoy®, can also be used to recover a MOB. Use a handybilly attached to the halyard or the halyard itself to lift the raft, complete with MOB, aboard the boat.

One of the advantages of this system is that it is much easier – and more comfortable for the MOB – to fasten the lifting rope to the raft than attaching to a MOB in the water. With practice the rafts are easy to get into and provide a horizontal lift. The disadvantage to using a Jonbuoy® is that the MOB has to be conscious in order to get into it.

MOB recovery on a motorboat is more difficult than on sailing yachts due to the lack of rigging.

Many motorcruisers carry a small inflatable dinghy in davits or on snap davits attached to the transom bathing ladder. A quick method of MOB recovery is to lower the dinghy and recover the MOB into the dinghy. Make sure helping crew are attached to the boat.

If the MOB is too heavy to lift into the dinghy, one of the sponsons can be deflated and the MOB rolled into the dinghy. Alternatively, launch a liferaft and pull the MOB into the raft. It may be necessary to partially deflate the upper tube of the raft.

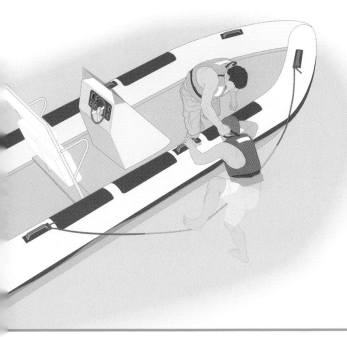

Getting a leg up

On small boats such as RIBs or sportsboats, a simple loop of line allows the MOB to help in their own recovery. The length needs to be just right – too short and the MOB will not be able to get their foot on to it, too long and the MOB will not be able to lift themselves high enough up the side of the boat.

Chapter 5
Be Seen – Detection Equipment

Radar reflectors and other target enhancers

Glassfibre boats are poor at reflecting radar signals and will often not show up on ships' radars. Since July 2002, it has been a requirement under SOLAS V to have on board a radar reflector or other means to enable detection by ships navigating by radar (if practicable to do so). The reflector should be capable of detection by ships navigating by radar at both 9 and 3 GHz, although detection on 3 GHz with a passive reflector is almost impossible.

The international standard that radar reflectors should meet is ISO 8729 – 1:2010.

Radar reflectors built to the current standard are often too large to be practically fitted to smaller vessels and it is with this in mind that the MCA have issued their guidance. They consider it to be feasible for vessels of 15m and over to fit radar reflectors that comply with the standard, but advise that vessels of under 15m in length should fit a radar reflector with the greatest echoing area practicable.

The MCA recommend that in addition to carrying a reflector it should be permanently installed and operational at all times, in accordance with the manufacturer's instructions.

The radar reflector should be mounted as high as possible on the boat, preferably at least 4m above sea level – so that it can be 'seen' from the greatest distance.

There are two basic types – passive radar reflectors and active radar target enhancers (RTEs).

Passive radar reflectors tend to be based either on standard corner reflector designs or lens designs. As a general rule of thumb, the bigger the reflector, the more likely it will be seen on a ship's radar. Most ships' radars automatically acquire the target using ARPA (Automatic Radar Plotting Aid). To do this, most require at least 50% of sweeps to be returned. Small radar reflectors usually do not provide sufficient returns for ARPA to work.

An octahedral reflector must be mounted in the 'catch rain' position for it to work as effectively as possible. Do not mount it from its points.

Many modern passive reflectors use 'stacked arrays' of corner reflectors held at different angles to increase reflectivity from as many directions around the boat and at different angles of heel. The arrays are housed inside plastic covers and are often mounted on the front of masts or hoisted in the rigging. Reflectors mounted on the front of a mast are likely to produce a radar shadow behind the mast, preventing them from returning the radar signal (A). Hanging them in the rigging provides a better all-round return. Radar reflectors work better when mounted vertically. Avoid mounting them at an angle, even though it may be more convenient.

Some passive reflectors use di-electric or Luneberg Lenses (B) and sometimes a combination of lenses and corner reflectors.

The lens is said to provide a more consistent response over greater angles, both horizontally and vertically, compared to corner reflectors, which may have large peaks and troughs. However, lens reflectors are often heavier than corner reflectors. Extra weight aloft may significantly affect a yacht's stability.

Active Radar Target Enhancers (C) are electronic devices that receive and then transmit back the radar frequency. Tests have shown these provide a large and consistent return and are, therefore, more likely to be 'seen' on radar than a passive radar reflector. The downside is that they rely on electrical power.

RTEs are now available with transmitters that respond either to 9GHz (X-band) radar only or to both 9GHz (3cm wavelength, X-band) and 3GHz (10cm wavelength, S-Band) radars.

A

B

C

Radar frequencies

Larger ships fit two types of radar – X-band and S-band. X-band transmit at a frequency of 9GHz while S-band transmit at 3GHz. Both will be operating at the same time when closing the coast and in busy waters.

The shorter wavelength of X-band radar gives it better definition and the ability to pick up smaller targets. It will also show rain, which can clutter the radar screen and possibly hide targets especially small ones such as boats.

S-band, on the other hand, is not hindered by rain but is less sensitive to smaller targets and the definition is not so exact.

When well out at sea, some ships will switch off their X-band sets, to save wear and tear, and use the S-band radar only.

Navigation lights

The navigation lights on your boat must comply with the very detailed specifications in the IRPCS (Colregs) (see page 16). It is illegal for vessels to use navigation lights that do not comply with these regulations. The following only provides a very basic overview of the requirements.

The COLREGs specify the lights a vessel must exhibit to indicate her navigational status at night and in restricted visibility. The rules are different for a vessel under power and a vessel under sail. The rules introduce alternative configurations that smaller vessels may exhibit in lieu, where the primary requirements are not practical.

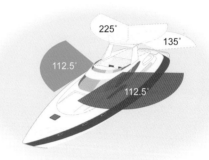

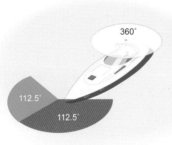

Less than 12m

Sailing vessels must be able to exhibit the lights for a power-driven vessel of the same size when motoring or motor sailing.

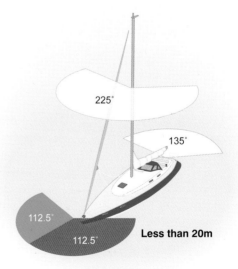

Less than 20m

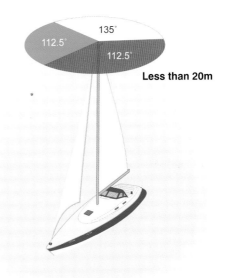

Vessels of less than 20m under sail may combine the sidelights and sternlight in one lantern at or near the top of the mast. This combined lantern must not be used when the vessel is under power as the masthead light required by a power-driven vessel must be at least 1m above the sidelights.

If it is not practical to exhibit the lights prescribed by the relevant rule, a power-driven vessel of less than 7m in length whose maximum speed does not exceed 7 knots may exhibit an all-round white light. A sailing vessel of less than 7m in length which cannot practically exhibit the required lights can rely on an electric torch or lighted lantern which it must show in sufficient time to avoid a collision. In practice a torch is also used in very small craft such as tenders even when powered by an outboard engine.

Vessels at anchor should show an all-round white light. If a boat under 7m in length is anchored away from a narrow channel, fairway, or anchorage and is away from where other vessels normally navigate, it is not required to do so.

Carry spare bulbs and other electrical spares in case your lights fail. Note that replacement LED lights may not provide the required colour for navigation lights.

Minimum visible range of lights

	Less than 12m	Over 12m less than 20m	Over 20m less than 50m
Masthead (steaming) light	2 miles	3 miles	5 miles
Stern light	2 miles	2 miles	2 miles
Port and starboard sidelights	1 mile	2 miles	2 miles

Check the light manufacturer's recommendations for the correct wattage bulb.

The danger of showing incorrect lights

Many power sports and speed boats have a permanently mounted bicolour light at the bow and a separate all-round white light on a short mast that is plugged into a deck socket close to the stern. Forget to fit the all-round light at night and, from ahead, the sports boat is showing the equivalent lights to a yacht under sail.

A small motor vessel seeing these lights approaching on their port side would assume that they should give way and pass to the stern. The sports boat skipper recognising the motor cruiser as the 'stand-on' vessel will also try to pass astern.

The consequence can lead to a collision.

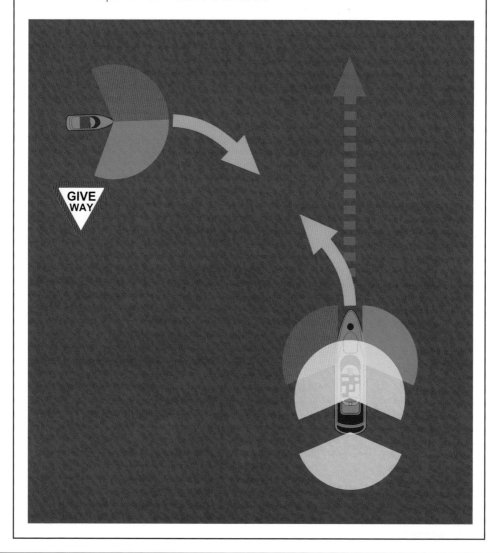

Day shapes

At anchor

When at anchor, power and sail boats should display a black ball in the forward part of the boat to show that they are anchored. For boats over 20m, the regulations require the ball to have a diameter no less than 0.6m. In smaller vessels, the ball's diameter should be commensurate with the size of the vessel.

The ball is usually made from two black plastic circles that slot together.

Boats under 7m not anchored in or near a narrow channel are exempt from this rule.

While it is easy to hoist a ball on a yacht, there's usually no provision for displaying an anchor ball on a motorboat. This can be simply rectified by mounting the ball on a suitable pole and placing into a deck socket, fitted into the foredeck, when needed.

Motorsailing

When motorsailing, sailing yachts are required to show an inverted cone in the forward section of the boat. This is so other craft will recognise that they are operating as a power craft rather than a yacht under sail and will apply the Colregs accordingly.

On boats over 20m, the base of the cone should be at least 0.6m and the height 0.6m. As with the anchor ball, on smaller vessels the cone should be commensurate with the size of the boat.

In some countries, motorsailing without an inverted cone can lead to prosecution.

Sound signals

Sound signals are prescribed by the collision regulations. They are used in four scenarios, manoeuvring, warning, in restricted visibility and for distress signalling. All vessels under 12m must have some way of making sound signals. For vessels over 12m, there are specific requirements for a 'whistle', a specific signal defined in the collision regulations, which for a boat up to 20m must be in the frequency range 180-700Hz ($\pm$1%).

A foghorn can be used to indicate your manoeuvring intentions – for example, turning to port, turning to starboard or which side you plan to overtake.

In confined navigational areas such as rivers it can be used as a warning when approaching a blind bend.

It can be used to indicate that you are unsure of another vessel's intentions. Continuously sounding the horn is a recognised distress signal.

Sound signals

1 blast = I am turning to starboard
2 blasts = I am turning to port
3 blasts = Engaged astern propulsion
5 blasts = Your intentions are unclear

IN FOG
Motorboat – one long blast at least every two minutes
Sail boat under sail – one long blast followed by two short blasts at least every two minutes

OVERTAKING
2 long blasts followed by one short = I intend to overtake on your starboard side
2 long blasts followed by two short = I intend to overtake on your port side.

Many boats carry gas horns. Some gas horns use heavier-than-air, inflammable gas such as butane – check the label on the gas can for the inflammable gas icon. Butane gas canisters must not be left in the sun either, for example, outside on a cockpit seat, or under a window or windscreen.

Take care when operating butane horns to prevent the gas from falling into the boat's bilges. Carry spare gas canisters. In tests, some gas foghorns provided less than an hour's worth of fog signals.

Be aware that the fog signal – one long and two short – used by craft under sail may not be possible with some gas horns since as the gas expands the horn diaphragm freezes and squeaks on the second and third blast.

Test your gas horn before you need it in fog. Ensure you buy a device capable of making the signals you need it to make.

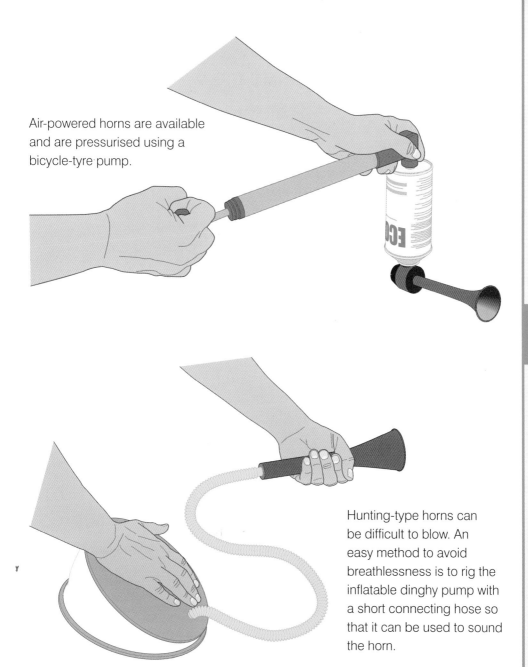

Air-powered horns are available and are pressurised using a bicycle-tyre pump.

Hunting-type horns can be difficult to blow. An easy method to avoid breathlessness is to rig the inflatable dinghy pump with a short connecting hose so that it can be used to sound the horn.

VHF Foghorn option

Many top-end leisure marine VHF radios now come with an electronic foghorn signal output that can be connected to an amplified loudspeaker or loud hailer. Choosing the appropriate sound signal in the VHF's operating menu will continually play the signal through the speaker at the correct intervals.

Chapter 6 Alternative Means of Propulsion and Steering

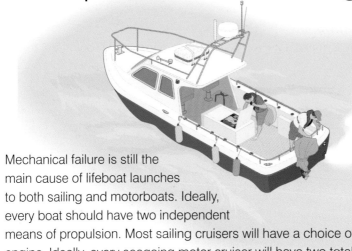

Mechanical failure is still the main cause of lifeboat launches to both sailing and motorboats. Ideally, every boat should have two independent means of propulsion. Most sailing cruisers will have a choice of sails and an auxiliary engine. Ideally, every seagoing motor cruiser will have two totally independent engines, each with its own isolated electrical and fuel systems.

If your boat has only one engine, be aware of the reliance you have on it for your safety. Correct regular maintenance is vital. If there is any doubt about the engine's reliability or condition, the problem must be resolved before setting out.

Smaller boats can usually fit or carry an auxiliary outboard. To fit an auxiliary outboard engine, it may be necessary to add an engine bracket to the boat's transom. It is likely it will need to have an extra-long leg to allow the propeller to sit low enough in the water without losing drive when the boat is pitching.

For boats from about 7m (23ft) to 30ft (9m), there are a number of yacht outboard engines from 6 to 10 hp designed to work at displacement speeds with extra-long legs and high-thrust propellers. Engines of this size may need to be permanently mounted in position. Even with smaller engines that are stowed below and moved into place when needed, make sure that you are able to lift the engine into place. Always fit a short lanyard between the engine and boat, just in case it slips out of your grasp.

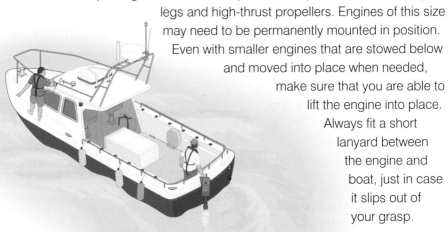

Before you need it in anger, check that you are able to start and operate your engine when it is in position. You may need to add an extension to the tiller. You may also need one of the crew to act as a lookout since it can be difficult or impossible to see when steering from the stern. The engine needs to be sufficiently powerful to push the boat in stronger weather – it's unlikely therefore on a larger boat that you would be able to use the tender's outboard.

In addition to the engine, make sure you carry sufficient fuel for the outboard, to get you back to a safe haven. Vessels over 9m tend to be too large or too heavy for an outboard to be of assistance. It is common for vessels over this size to have two engines in the case of powerboats.

Small boats up to 5m can be propelled using paddles or oars but they are only effective in good conditions and for as long as the paddlers can paddle.

Fuel consumption

Boats consume much greater levels of fuel than cars. It is normal for a planing motor cruiser to have a fuel consumption of 1 mile per gallon (mpg) or less, at full throttle. While reducing throttle to cruising speed does reduce consumption it is still likely to be around the 2 to 3 miles per gallon mark.

Semi-displacement boats, sportsboats and RIBs will achieve a consumption in the region of 2 to 5 mpg.

Displacement boats and sailing yachts under power provide the best fuel consumption figures – expect in the region of 6 to 12 mpg.

Calculate your own boat's fuel consumption. Base it on engine revolutions not boat speed since speed will change depending on the sea conditions. Most engine manufacturers can provide figures as a starting guide.

A rough guide to consumption...
■ Two stroke engines – 1 gallon per hour per 10hp
■ Four stroke engines – 1 gallon per hour per 15hp
■ Diesel engines – 1 gallon per hour per 20hp
(Note: 1 gallon is equal to 4.5 litres)
For example a 100hp two stroke outboard is likely to burn 100/10 = 10 gallons per hour at full throttle. These calculations err on the side of safety and slightly over estimate consumption.

Use the Thirds Rule to ensure you have sufficient fuel.

One-third of capacity to get there, one-third of capacity to get back and one-third spare to cope with changes in conditions and other unforeseen circumstances. Some skippers that are towed in will blame it on the engine breaking down when in reality they have simply run out of fuel. If carrying an auxiliary engine that runs on different fuel to your main engine, ensure you have sufficient fuel for the auxiliary to get you to safety. If the same fuel is used for both engines, consider ways of connecting the auxiliary to the main engine's supply.

If the auxiliary is a two stroke petrol engine, carry sufficient 2-stroke oil.

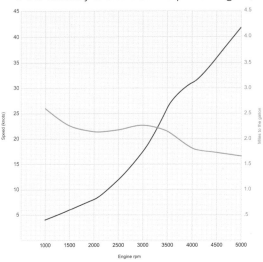

Most diesel engine manufacturers produce consumption figures for their engine which you can use to give you an estimate of your boat's fuel consumption at different engine speeds (rpm). For the technically minded sailor, you can relate your boat speed to the engine rpm and draw up speed and consumption curves. From the curves, you can quickly see your most economical cruising speed.

Using the boat speed and consumption per hour (lt/hr) figures, you can estimate your boat's range and fuel consumption per hour. The range curve will look similar in shape to the lt/hour or gallons/hour curve.

To calculate miles per gallon at a particular engine rpm, divide the boat's speed in knots (nautical miles per hour) by the gallons per hour figure. To calculate Range, on the basis of the thirds rule, multiply the tank capacity in gallons or litres by 0.66, divide by either the gallons/hour or litres/hour figure and multiply by the boat's speed.

Some people like to know the number of litres/hour is likely to be burnt at a particular speed. This can be calculated by dividing the lts/hour figure by the speed.

These figures will give you an estimate of consumption (and running costs!)
Remember that weather and wave
conditions will change your boat's consumption.

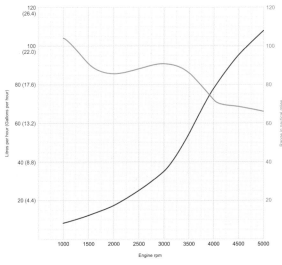

It's not unusual for a motor cruiser to consume fuel at the rate of 1 mile/gallon (or more) at cruising speed. Sailing yachts and other displacement boats are likely to consume at the rate of about 6 to 12 mpg.

Alternative starting

A flat battery will not be able to start an engine. Batteries can be flattened by over use of the domestic systems such as the fridge or lights.

Outboard engines up to about 50 to 60hp can be started by accessing the flywheel and attaching a pull-start rope. Only use the cord that is supplied by the manufacturer.

On small engines, it may be possible to hand crank the engine. Check there is sufficient room to turn the handle and practise starting the engine before you need to do it in an emergency.

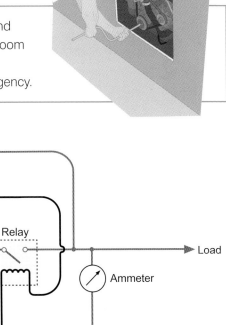

You can have a twin battery system that reserves one battery solely for engine starting. There are several alternatives. The system can be as simple as a three-way switch that allows the batteries to be used individually or together. One alternative is to wire a relay or blocking diode system that allows the engine to charge both batteries but only allows one to be used for domestics supply.

Propeller rope cutters

With the large amount of
flotsam and jetsam plus
the large number of poorly
marked lobster pots, a rope
cutter can prevent the boat
from becoming snagged and
the possibility of significant
damage.

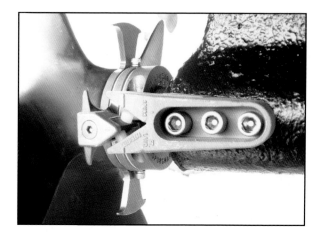

Rope cutters fit on to the
shaft in front of the propeller
and are designed to cut rope,
netting or plastic sheet to
prevent it becoming entangled
around the propeller, which would cause a loss of propulsion, stop and, possibly,
damage the engine.

There are two basic types – scissor style, as shown here, and disc types that
consist of a sharpened disc and use the propeller blades to drag the rope over the
edge of the blade.

Avoid donning a dive mask, fins and wetsuit (or scuba gear) and going over the
side to cut the debris clear. It's better to call for help. However, if there is no
alternative, it should only be considered if the sea is calm. Never go under
a pitching and heaving boat. The safety of the individual should never
be compromised.

An advantage of outboard engines is that they can be tilted to
allow access to the propeller. Always ensure that the boat's
painter is shorter than the length of the boat to prevent it
snagging around the propeller with the
engine down.

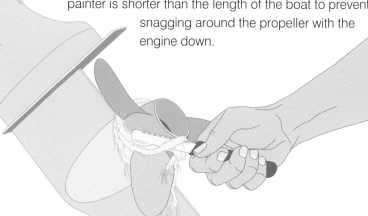

Engine spares

No leisure skipper or crew would be expected to repair a major problem with their boat's engine when at sea. However, there are a number of smaller 'first aid' problems that can be dealt with without resorting to calling the emergency services. However, these will require some spares to be carried on board.

The RYA's one day Diesel Engine Course is extremely useful and covers basic maintenance and simple fault-finding and repairs.

Most engine makers will provide a set of onboard spares, which you can add to and adapt as necessary.

Suggested engine spares include:

■ Engine and gearbox oil (sufficient for a complete oil change)

■ Drive belts

■ Water pump impellers and gaskets

■ Fuel filter elements

■ Oil filter elements

■ Engine fuses

■ Spark plugs (for petrol engines)

■ Kill cords

■ Outboard engine fuel line

■ Hoses and hose clips

■ Diesel bug treatment

On a longer trip you may need a more extensive spares kit so do you have the bits an engineer might otherwise need to order?

Electrical spares

Carry replacement bulbs for navigation lights, spare batteries for every item of equipment that needs them, spare fuses for the distribution panel (many panels are now fitted with circuit breakers) and distilled water for lead-acid batteries.

A hydrometer, to check the state of charge of lead-acid batteries, a simple electrical circuit tester or multimeter and various lengths of wire may also come in useful.

Tool kit

You need the tools to be able to undertake the jobs you can do at sea or in a port away from home in order to get the boat going again. See G87 RYA Offshore Sailing for further information.

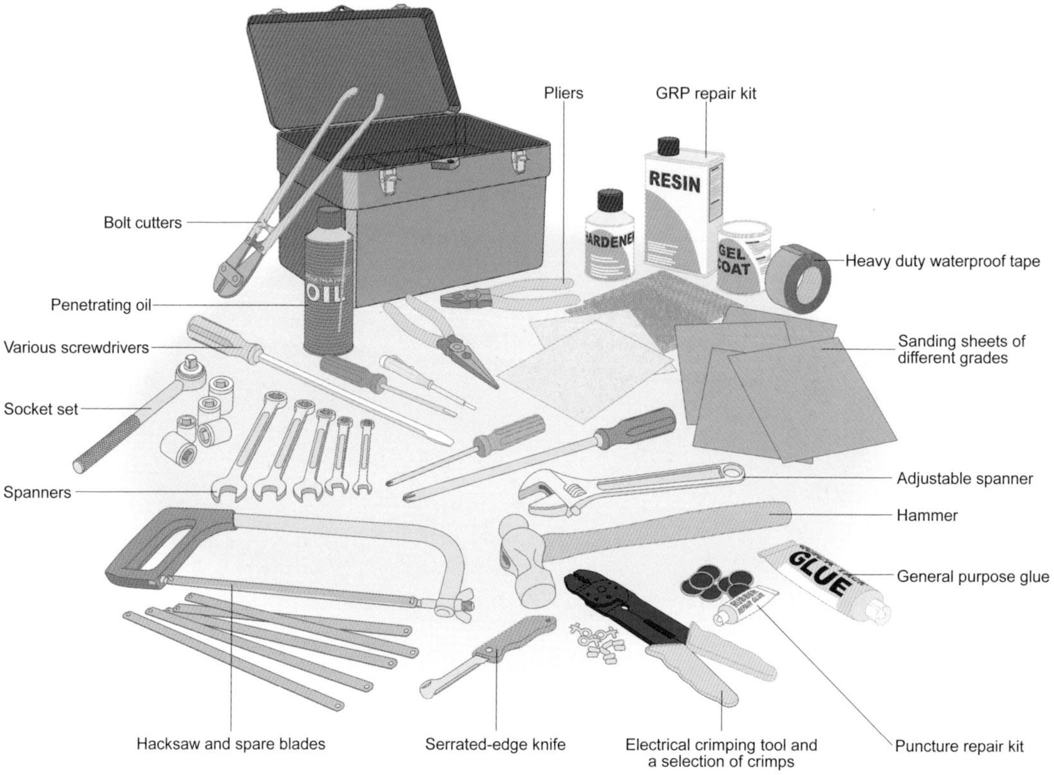

See G87 RYA Offshore Sailing

Pliers

GRP repair kit

RESIN

HARDENER

GEL COAT

Bolt cutters

Heavy duty waterproof tape

Penetrating oil

Various screwdrivers

Sanding sheets of different grades

Socket set

Spanners

Adjustable spanner

Hammer

GLUE

General purpose glue

Hacksaw and spare blades

Serrated-edge knife

Electrical crimping tool and a selection of crimps

Puncture repair kit

Emergency steering

Steering failures fall into two categories. Those caused by a breakage in the steering connections to the rudder or outboard and those that involve the complete loss of the rudder. How you deal with them will depend on the problem and the type of boat.

By being able to steer the boat you can start heading back towards help and cut the towing time to a minimum. If far offshore, they may be no other option.

Some possible solutions to broken steering connection

Some systems are supplied with an emergency tiller that fits to the top of the rudder stock. Check that it fits and there's sufficient space to turn it. Can you see where you are going or will you need a lookout?

On an inboard/outboard engine's outdrive, disconnect the steering link and fasten one or two lines to the outdrive tiller. Use the lines to steady and direct the outdrive. You will probably need to take a couple of turns around grab handle stanchions to cope with the propeller's torque. Twin propellers should have minimal torque.

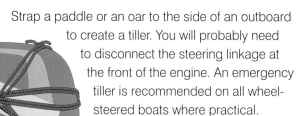

Strap a paddle or an oar to the side of an outboard to create a tiller. You will probably need to disconnect the steering linkage at the front of the engine. An emergency tiller is recommended on all wheel-steered boats where practical.

Rudder gone?

First check there's no water entering the boat through the rudder stock hole. Bung the hole (see page 143) to reduce or stop the water flow, man the pumps and call for help.

On a sailing yacht, by carefully balancing the forces in the sails, it is possible to steer the boat. It takes practice and, of course, unless you have a fold-up rudder, the underwater geometry won't be the same as when the rudder's there but you will be able to get a feel for how the boat handles and perfect the techniques.

Wind blowing onto the mainsail

Stern pushed round

Pivot around keel

All rudder control gone

Bow thrusters

Many larger boats are now fitted with bow thrusters. Short bursts may be enough to keep you pointing in the right direction.

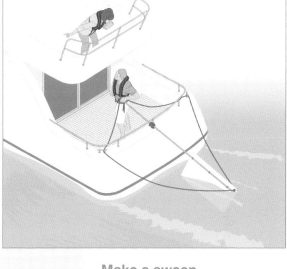

The foresail has been made to flog which has moved the centre of lateral resistance back because the mainsail is the only sail providing any force and the boat pivots around the keel. This forces the stern around and the boat starts to move towards the wind effectively steering the boat without a rudder. The opposite effect is achieved by flogging the mainsail and hardening the foresail so even without a rudder the boat can be steered with sail trim only.

Make a sweep

With a little bit of prior preparation it can be possible to jury rig a sweep, be it to a motor cruiser or sailing yacht. Use a sturdy boathook, a whisker or a spinnaker pole and a floorboard or bunk board. Pre-drill the board with holes so that it can be lashed to the pole. Pivot the improvised sweep on the transom with another lashing and support the board with a knotted warp.

Other techniques

A bucket or a drogue on a bridle over the stern of the boat can increase the drag on one or other side of the boat to make her turn. If the rudder is stuck amidships, body weight can be used on small craft – simply move the crew from one side of the boat and back to the middle. The extra drag on one side will cause the boat to turn.

Jury rigs/rigging spares

Avoid a mast breakage by watching out for broken strands and cracks in the standing rigging. Standing rigging deteriorates with age and should be inspected regularly. Replacement times will depend on the amount and type of use the vessel experiences.

If the mast should come down, cut it away, freeing the clevis pins from the rigging to deck fittings. Carry on board some means for severing the rigging. Bolt croppers can cope with most stainless steel rigging up to about 8mm diameter. Above that size and with rod rigging you will need a ratchet or hydraulic cutter or a Shoot-It® wire cutter that uses Hilti® cartridges to drive a cutting knife through the wire.

A hacksaw can be used but it may be difficult to hold the wire or fitting steady. For stainless steel use a silicon carbide blade.

Save what you can for making a jury rig to get you back to safety.

Suggested kit of spares and tools for maintaining the rig.

Bosun's chair

Sail batten

Rigging wire

Halyard

Block

Various length and diameter sheets

Winch handle

Thread, palm and needles

Twine and small cordage

Thimbles and wire clamps

Metal shackles and split pins

Hanks, sail slides and shackles

Storm sails

For sailing yachts going offshore, a storm jib and trysail can provide enough drive to keep the yacht head to sea without overpowering the boat.

Storm sails need to be set up before the worst of the weather hits while it's still possible to work safely on deck.

Brightly coloured so that they can be easily seen, the storm jib can be rigged in a variety of ways, including to an inner forestay or with proprietary 'socks' that fit over a rolled headsail to allow the sail to be hanked on to the main forestay.

The trysail replaces the mainsail and is (usually) sheeted through blocks at the stern. The boom is lowered and lashed to the coachroof.

Both sails are made of very heavy duty material with extra strong clews. A temporary inner forestay, tensioned with a forestay lever, can be rigged on to a deck eye in the middle of the foredeck.

It's best to have a separate track on the mast and, preferably, a spare halyard for setting the trysail. The track should come well down the mast below the boom's goose neck so that the trysail sliders can be put on to the track so that the sail is ready to be hoisted. Keep the trysail in its sail bag, fastened to the bottom of the mast, with the spare halyard attached to the head of the sail but secure. The sheets are led aft through pulleys attached to the stern and back forward to the sheet winches. If a boat is fitted with lazy jacks these will need to be secured out of the way of the trysail.

Many cruising sailors argue that having a deep third or fourth reef point to reduce significantly the mainsail area removes the need for trysails. Although this is true from a reducing sail area angle, it doesn't give you the option of having a purely independent storm sail to set.

Trysail

Storm jib

Preventers for downwind sailing

To prevent an accidental gybe a preventer can be rigged when downwind sailing. It's essential that the preventer is led back to the cockpit so that it can be released quickly. Poling out the headsail will provide more drive.

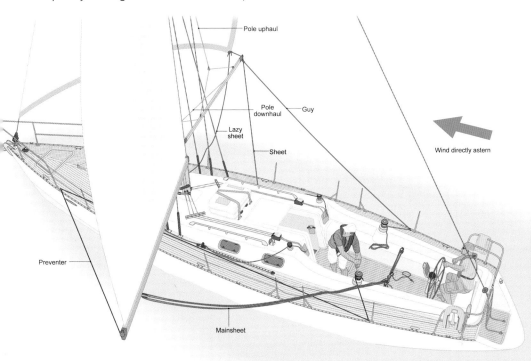

Pole uphaul

Pole downhaul

Guy

Lazy sheet

Sheet

Wind directly astern

Preventer

Mainsheet

Towing/mooring warp and fenders

Carry a long strong rope to use for towing – at least 30m in length on smaller craft. Select a rope with a diameter appropriate to the length and weight of your vessel. The warp can also be used to trail astern in following seas to prevent broaching. It may be possible to use the kedge anchor warp for towing duties.

Mooring warp and fenders will be needed for an alongside tow.

Always spread the load of the tow to several cleats and, if need be, around the stern of the vessel.

Chapter 7 Calling for Help

There are several different ways for calling for help. But for the modern sailor, electronic means are usually the first option.

The Global Maritime Distress and Safety System, implemented in February 1999, sets out a world-wide co-ordinated approach to calling for help. Merchant vessels are required under the scheme to carry at least two independent means of radio distress alerting. The system also provides for urgency and safety communications and for the provision of navigational and weather warnings.

Leisure craft are not required to fit GMDSS-compatible equipment but are encouraged to do so.

The type of equipment suggested depends on where you sail. The GMDSS divides the world into four areas.

■ Area A1 – within range of a shore-based VHF coast station fitted with DSC (up to 50 miles depending on antenna height).
■ Area A2 – within range of shore-based MF coast station fitted with DSC (up to about 100 to 300 miles).
■ Area A3 – between latitudes 70 degrees N and 70 degrees S.
■ Area A4 – North and south of 70 degrees N and 70 degrees S. I.e. the polar regions.

Equipment covered by GMDSS includes – VHF, MF/HF SSB, Inmarsat A/B, C and M, Navtex, EPIRBs, PLBs and SARTs.

VHF radio

For most boat owners sailing in area A1 a marine VHF is the first method of raising the alarm.

Fixed marine VHF transceivers offered for sale in the UK must meet the technical requirements of the European Radio and Telecommunications Terminal Equipment Directive (R&TTE) standard EN301205. Second hand sets and those bought overseas often do not meet the required standard and may be fitted with incorrect radio channels.

All new fixed sets have to be compatible with DSC (Digital Selective Calling). Most have DSC controllers built into the radio. DSC is a major part of the GMDSS. DSC sets are fitted with a dedicated distress button that, in a matter of seconds, will alert the rescue services and other shipping within VHF range. The alert will tell them who you are, where you are and that you need help. DSC also reduces routine radio traffic on Ch16 making it easier to hear voice distress calls.

For a DSC radio to work effectively, it needs to be connected to a GPS receiver so that its position information is updated every second.

The range of the radio is mainly determined by the height of the transmitting and receiving antennas. As a guide, a 10m yacht should be able to broadcast and receive to a shore station up to 25 to 30 miles away while a sports boat to sports boat call is likely to be in the region of 5 miles.

Handheld VHF radios

Portable handheld VHF radios are less powerful than fixed transceivers. Virtually all do not have DSC capability – although a new handheld VHF with DSC is now available on the market.

On smaller boats it may not be practical to fit a fixed VHF. A handheld VHF may be a useful alternative and is certainly a better option than no VHF at all. A handheld VHF is also useful as a back-up to a fixed VHF and can of course be taken in the tender or the liferaft.

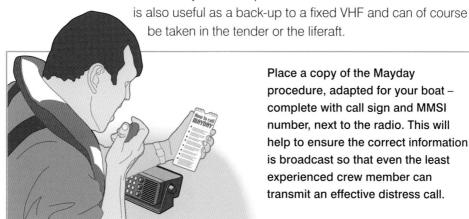

Place a copy of the Mayday procedure, adapted for your boat – complete with call sign and MMSI number, next to the radio. This will help to ensure the correct information is broadcast so that even the least experienced crew member can transmit an effective distress call.

Licensing

Ship

All vessels fitted with radio equipment are required to have a valid Ship Radio Licence. In the UK , this is provided by Ofcom – contact details on page 157 – free of charge when applying on line (postal applications require a fee). The Ship Radio Licence is for the life of the vessel but owners are required to renew the licence every 10 years.

When the licence is issued for the first time, the boat will be given a call sign and, if fitted with a DSC radio, an MMSI (Maritime Mobile Service Identity) number.

Handheld VHF radios which are not part of a boat's inventory also have to be licensed. These require a Ship Portable Radio Licence.

Operator

Without a maritime radio operator's certificate, a VHF radio may be monitored for safety purposes or used to summon assistance in a distress situation, but it may not be used for general transmissions. General transmissions can only be made by a licensed operator or by someone under the direct supervision of a licensed operator. The Short Range Certificate is the most common operator's certificate which covers the use of VHF and VHF/DSC equipment. The SRC is available through RYA recognised training centres.

Emergency antenna

If the antenna is damaged, such as in a dismasting on a sailing yacht or an MOB grabbing at the aerial as they fell off the side of a motor cruiser, the VHF will not be able to broadcast for help. An emergency VHF antenna can be rigged to replace it. Most are telescopic and pack away in a small easily stowed tube. You will need to be able to gain access to the back of the VHF set to connect the antenna.

VHF versus Mobile phone

A mobile phone can be used to call for help but it is a poor substitute for a marine VHF for several reasons...

- VHF radios have a greater range

- A VHF alerts all in range. A DSC set will trigger all other DSC sets in range to sound a loud alarm

- SAR services can triangulate the position of a VHF transmission and can home in on the signal

- VHFs have a longer battery life

- Distress calls can be sent in seconds (DSC)

- Mobile phones are designed for land use. They have poor coverage at sea and reduced range

- They only alert the person you call.

- The emergency services operator will be the first one available and maybe located anywhere in the country. It will take time to determine your position and which Maritime Rescue Co-ordination Centre (Coastguard) to connect you with.

- If VHF is not available in inshore waters a mobile phone is, at least, better than nothing.

Use the national emergency services number. In the UK, dial 999 (or 112 throughout Europe, 911 in the USA) and ask for the Coastguard.

AIS SART and AIS Personal Locator Beacons

An AIS SART (search and rescue transmitter) is similar to a SART (search and rescue (radar) transponder) in so much that it is a small float-free device designed to indicate the position of a vessel, liferaft or casualties in the water.

Unlike a SART, which responds to receiving a radar transmission – see page 89, the AIS SART transmits on the AIS frequencies an identification code and position – calculated from an integral GPS – which can be picked up by an AIS receiver and shown on a chart plotter or radar screen capable of accepting AIS information. If the screen is using the latest chart plotting protocol, the AIS SART will be shown as a red circle with a cross in it.

The AIS SART continually transmits an updated signal every minute. Once triggered, it will broadcast for up to 96 hours. A similar device, the AIS personal locator beacon, works in a similar way but is smaller, so that it can be easily carried, and transmits for a shorter period – usually 24 hours.

Satellite mobile phones

Satellite phones are becoming popular with offshore sailors as an alternative to SSB (single sideband) radio. Their worldwide range allows yachtsmen to call rescue services anywhere in the world. Remember to store Coastguard Rescue Co-ordination centres' telephone numbers into the phone's directory.

Long range radio

For sailors on extended voyages and beyond the range of VHF (about 20 to 30 nautical miles (NM) depending on antenna height), Single Side Band (SSB) medium frequency (MF) radios – frequencies between 300kHz and 3MHz – and high frequency (HF) radios – frequencies between 3MHz and 30MHz – provide greater range.

Using ground wave propagation, where the signal follows the curvature of the Earth, MF can often transmit over several hundred miles. Normally, a typical range for reliable transmissions for an MF coast station is up to 300NM while a ship station could expect a range up to 150NM due to its less powerful and smaller antenna.

By reflecting off higher levels of the ionosphere, HF ranges can be considerably greater – up to many thousands of miles dependant on the atmospheric conditions and the quality of the installation of the HF set.

The boat needs to be properly set up, something that would normally require professional help, and would usually include an insulated back-stay antenna, an antenna tuner unit and a good grounding system in addition to the transmitter itself. As well as voice messages, the system can be linked to a computer via a pactor modem, to send short email messages – useful for keeping in touch with home or ordering parts so that they are ready for arrival at a destination. It can also be set up to receive weatherfax.

To use an MF or HF radio, a non-professional operator needs to hold the Long Range Certificate.

The distress and emergency frequency used for voice communications on MF is 2182KHz – the equivalent of Ch 16 on VHF – while the HF marine distress voice frequencies are 4125, 6215, 8291, 12290 and 16420kHz.

As with VHF, MF and HF alerts can also be sent via Digital Selective Calling. On MF the DSC frequency is 2187.5kHz. On HF, there is a choice of, 4207.5, 6312, 8414.5, 12577 and 16804.5kHz. These frequencies are reserved solely for distress, urgency and safety alerts.

The choice of frequency to use depends on the location of the boat. In Sea Area A2, the alert should be sent on 2187.5kHz. In Sea Area A3, the alert should be sent on 8414.5kHz and all other HF DSC frequencies.

SSB radios offer low running costs for long range communication compared to mobile and satellite communication systems and are therefore popular with blue-sea cruising yachtsmen.

EPIRBs

Transmitting on frequencies of 406MHz and 121.5MHz, Emergency Position Indicating Radio Beacons alert the rescue services by sending a distress signal via Inmarsat and Cospas-Sarsat satellites.

The four Inmarsat satellites circle the Earth in a geostationary orbit and cover an area from about 70 degrees North to 70 degrees South. They immediately forward the distress message to a ground station.

Cospas-Sarsat satellites are in lower orbits that travel over the poles. They circle the Earth approximately every 12 hours and will either retransmit the distress alert to a ground station immediately or hold on to it until a ground station comes into 'view'.

Both sets of satellites will react to all 406MHz EPIRB distress alerts.

Two types of EPIRB are available – those with either a built-in, or linked to, GPS and those without. EPIRBs must be registered with the EPIRB registry in the country of their vessel's flag and may require programming with an ID code.

GPS EPIRB – provides a distress alert (if within the Inmarsat area) and a position accurate to 100m within five minutes.

Standard EPIRB – provides distress alert within five minutes if the Earth station is within the satellite range and position to within 3 nautical miles (5Km) within 40 minutes to two hours depending on your location.

Built-in to the EPIRB is a 121.5MHz beacon. SAR craft will use radio direction finders to home into the signal as they close on to the casualty.

EPIRBs can be activated manually or automatically on contact with the sea.

Float free versions – known as Category 1 EPIRBs, are mounted outside and use a hydrostatic release unit to release the device when the boat sinks to a depth of 4 metres. Category 2 EPIRBs are designed to be removed manually from a bracket and should be stowed, on a bracket, inside the boat, close to the cabin exit.

Built to SOLAS standards, EPIRBs have a battery life of 48 hours, float upright when in the water and are fitted with a strobe light so that they can be seen at night and lanyard to attach it to a liferaft or casualty.

Batteries have a life of 5 years and must be replaced when specified. Some EPIRBs do not allow battery replacements and should be de-activated and safely disposed of when the battery has to be renewed.

An EPIRB can be hired if only occasionally travelling long distances offshore. Contact an EPIRB manufacturer or distributor for details.

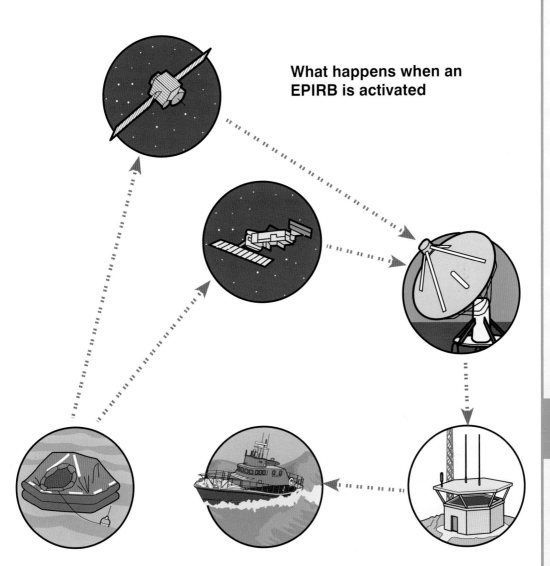

What happens when an EPIRB is activated

When the EPIRB is activated, it transmits a signal via satellite to an earth station. The earth station sends it to the appropriate Rescue Co-Ordination Centre or Mission Control Centre who will task a ship or local rescue services to your position.

TIP

When transporting an EPIRB it is advisable to wrap the device in aluminium foil and place inside a metal container to prevent an accidental alert.

PLBs

Sometimes referred to as PEPIRBs, Personal Locator Beacons are, in effect, smaller versions of EPIRBs, and are carried by individual crew or in grab bags. Where they differ is they are not designed to float free in an upright position and transmit automatically from the water – they must be triggered manually. Additionally, some may not be buoyant, they may not have an internal strobe light, their battery is designed to allow transmission for at least 24 hours (some provide 48 hours), and the antenna must be held in a vertical position.

As with EPIRBs, there are two 406MHz PLB types – GPS PLB and a Standard PLB. They provide identical response times and positional accuracy to their EPIRB cousins.

Also built into the PLB is a 121.5MHz homing beacon. SAR craft use radio direction finders to home in to the signal.

Most countries require 406MHz PLBs to be registered.

121.5 PLBs

Worn by individual crew, 121.5 PLBs can trigger an on board alarm to alert crew that somebody has gone over the side. A radio direction finder, carried by search & rescue vessels, can also be used to home in on the MOB. Always tell the SAR services if a MOB may be using a 121.5MHz PLB.

The antenna needs to be held as high as possible to give the greatest range.

SARTs

A Search and Rescue Radar Transponder is an alerting and position finding electronic device that produces a distinctive 'echo' on the screen of any 9GHz (X-band) radar. Previously only fitted to commercial vessels' liferafts, SARTs are now sufficiently small to be carried on board a boat or fitted as an optional extra in a leisure liferaft.

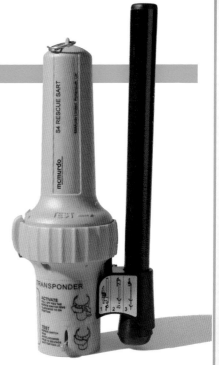

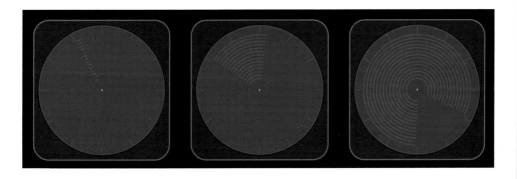

| Fig. 1 | Fig. 2 | Fig. 3 |

Fig. 1: The SART starts transmitting when it receives a radar signal. On initial contact with a SART, the receiving radar will show a line of dots giving range and direction to the casualty. The nearest dot is the casualty's position.

Fig. 2: As the radar closes on the SART, the dots broaden to arcs at about 2 to 3 miles range.

Fig 3: When the arcs make an almost complete circle the SART is within 1 mile.

Range depends on the height of the SART and the height of the radar scanner. A SAR helicopter at 1000m (3000ft) can pick up a SART at 48 miles while a boat radar 7m above the waterline will detect the SART at about 6 miles.

Inmarsat-C and Mini-C systems

Normally fitted to larger trans-oceanic vessels, Inmarsat-C/Mini-C is a digital satellite communications system that can transmit and receive anything that can be encoded into a digital format – email, fax, instrument data and tracking information for example. Known as a store and forward messaging system, it broadcasts data via the Inmarsat satellites to Land Earth Stations (LES) in 'packages' where it is reassembled and sent on to the addressee.

Distress alerting, sent as a priority message, and marine safety information broadcasts can be sent and received. The sets can be linked to, or include, a GPS to provide position information.

Coverage is virtually worldwide but excludes the poles.

Part of the Inmarsat-C service is a sort of Inmarsat version of Navtex. Called SafetyNET, it provides marine safety information for vessels travelling beyond the reach of Navtex. It is broadcast as part of an Enhanced Group Call (EGC). The service provider determines which sets are to receive the message by including identifying information, such as the navarea/metarea/geographical area for which the MSI is intended. Additionally, it is not free. The safety information service is free but there is a data transfer fee charged per character to receive it.

Inmarsat Fleet Broadband 505

Launched in 2007, Inmarsat Fleet Broadband offers a satellite-based telephone and broadband system that can be used on relatively small vessels. Unlike Inmarsat-C, it's not part of the GMDSS system but uses the same satellites, located in geostationary orbit at a height of 22,236 miles, and therefore like Inmarsat-C, is limited in operation between 72°N and 72°S.

Although relatively slow compared to shore-based broadband, Fleet Broadband offers hitherto unavailable access to broadband for small vessels at sea. It is available in 150, 284 and 432kbps (kilobytes per second). The antennas for the systems are relatively small and light – about 2kg and measuring in the region of 290mm. In addition to the initial purchase prices, which, at the time of writing in 2011, start at over £3000 there is also an airtime charge depending on the service used from under a US$ for a sms message to US$40 for the highest level of broadband access.

The advantages of broadband access while at sea are obvious – information such as weather and wave height that is available ashore becomes available when on the water – let alone the ability to email friends, family and harbours of your imminent arrival.

In addition to broadband, internet telephone voice call facilities are also provided.

As part of the service, a no-cost dedicated emergency number – 505 – has been allocated for making distress or urgency calls. By dialling 505, the ship is connected direct to the nearest of three Maritime Rescue Co-ordination Centres (MRCCs) strategically located across the globe. 505 was chosen because of its similarity in appearance to SOS.

Flares

Although traditionally flares were one of the primary devices for requesting assistance in a distress situation, EPIRBs, PLBs and DSC VHF (if carried) are now likely to be the first line of defence. Where an EPIRB, PLB or DSC VHF is carried on a vessel of less than 13.7m in length, the RYA no longer considers it to be essential also to carry the full complement of flares previously required. A minimum of 4 handheld red flares is, however, still recommended to allow a vessel to be located by the rescuer in the final few miles. Always make sure that you have read and understood the manufacturer's instructions before use.

Check your boat insurance remains valid if you do decide not to carry flares – some insurance companies have been known to void a claim because of the lack of correct safety equipment.

Stow flares, where they will be easily accessible, in a waterproof container. Line the container with sponge foam or bubble wrap to protect them from knocks and bumps. Do not pack in polystyrene chips since it can make it difficult to find the correct flare easily in an emergency.

Make sure the container's lid is not fastened so tight that others can't open it or, indeed, if you have injured your hand or arm.

The number and type of flares to carry are shown in the table on page 17.

Commercial flare packs do not always have the recommended number and type of flares. Race rules often specify a minimum pack.

Which distress flare?

Red handheld flare
– burns for at least
one minute at 15,000
candela. Visible up to 7
miles. Use day or night.

Red parachute rocket flare – fires up
to a height of at least 300 metres and
burns for at least 40 seconds at 30,000
candela. Visible for up to 28 miles. Use
day or night.

**Buoyant orange
smoke** – produces
bright orange smoke
for over three minutes.
Visible up to 7 miles.
Use during daylight only. Can be used to
mark MOB.

**Handheld orange
smoke** – produces
bright orange smoke
for at least one minute.
Visible up to 7 miles.
Use during daylight only. Not to SOLAS
standard.

Day/night flare
– personal flare,
waterproof. Used by
divers, RNLI crew
and, increasingly,
boat users. Has a
smoke flare at one end and a red flare
at other end. Each end burns for 18 to
20 seconds. Visible up to 7 miles. Not to
SOLAS standard.

**Personal distress
signal** – personal
aerial flare fires a small
red flare cartridge up to
heights of 45m or 90m
depending on make.
Comes in packs of
three or nine cartridges.
Burns for about 5
to 6 seconds. Fire two cartridges in
succession. Visible up to 15 miles at
night, 10 miles during day. Not to SOLAS
standard. Cartridges also available in
other colours from some manufacturers.

Non-distress flares

Handheld white flares raise awareness and pinpoint position to other shipping to
prevent collision. Stow white anti-collision flares where they are easily accessible – in
clips in the companionway, or next to the helm, but out of reach of young children.
Since most are the same shape and size to red distress flares, it's best to keep them
separate.

White parachute rocket flares are used to illuminate the local area at night. Good for
searching for MOB.

Handling flares

There should be a two second delay after pulling the string of a handheld flare, Don't be tempted to look into the end of the flare if it does not fire immediately. If a flare fails to fire, either if possible immerse in bucket of water or throw overboard. If you are using flares then you are already in enough trouble – a flare going off accidentally will only make things worse.

As a general rule always stand with your back to the wind when firing flares. Handheld red flares usually produce copious amounts of ash and dross and occasionally will spit out red-hot embers. Always hold them at an angle over the leeward side of the boat or liferaft. Red and white handheld flares burn with the intensity of the light of an arc welder. Look away, particularly at night, so as not to lose your night vision. Leather gloves (gardening gloves) are not required but can provide extra confidence when using flares so long as they still allow you to grip the flare firmly.

Flare Disposal

Time-expired pyrotechnics or out-of-date (OOD) flares should be disposed of safely. They are not fireworks and should not be used as part of a firework display – even when well inland. Parachute rocket flares have been known not to extinguish before they land and can set fire to anything they land on.

In the UK, HM Coastguard has taken on the responsibility of accepting OOD flares. Previously, old flares could be handed in at a Coastguard Sector Office, but since 1 April 2010 they will only accept them by appointment at one of their approved centres around the UK and Northern Ireland. The RNLI also accept OOD flares at their headquarters in Poole, Dorset.

For many people that may mean a round trip of several hours. While it might be tempting to take several people's OOD flares, take care not to carry too many flares in your car and thereby break transport regulations and invalidate your car insurance.

To make an appointment, you will need to phone the centre first. Be ready to give details of the type, quantity, age and condition of the flare.

It is illegal to put OOD flares in general rubbish. Firing a flare in a non-distress situation is liable to a fine of up to £2000.

Never fire a rocket or mini flare when aircraft are overhead.

Rescue lasers

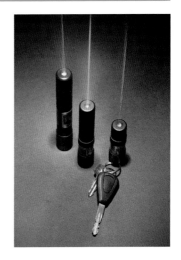

Due to the limited life span for pyrotechnic flares and the difficulties of their disposal, the authorities are now considering the use of rescue lasers. However, they are not currently recognised as an official distress signal.

These are designed to replace handheld (location) flares that are used to identify and indicate a vessel or person in distress.

There are two types – one that has to be pointed at the potential rescuer – use your fingers in the same way as using a heliograph to aim the laser – and the other provides an all-round light (similar to pyrotechnic flare) by rotating four laser lights.

It is claimed that the light can be seen up to 30 miles in optimal conditions at night and up to 3 miles in daylight and are safe if used correctly. But a word of caution: do not be tempted to use a presentation laser pointer as an alternative since these can damage eyesight.

Concerns have been raised during trials that shining a rescue laser during the hours of darkness at helicopter pilots using night vision goggles can cause the goggles to flare out for up to three minutes.

Using a heliograph (mirror or CD)

A heliograph is a simple way of drawing attention. Some come with a short stick and string but you can use your hand instead.

With one eye, look through the hole in the middle. Hold up your fingers and use them as a sight. Angle the mirror to reflect light on to the fingers. The target will see the twinkling reflection off the mirror. Practise with a CD but be aware that the shiny surface will dissolve in water.

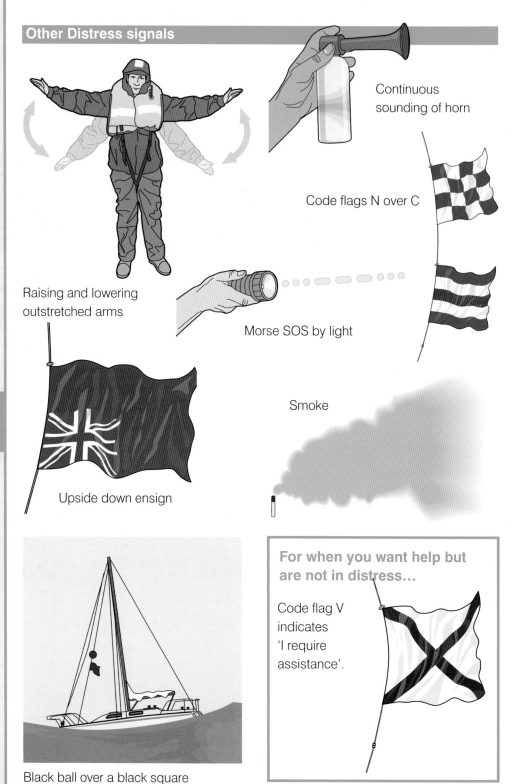

Continuous sounding of horn

Code flags N over C

Raising and lowering outstretched arms

Morse SOS by light

Smoke

Upside down ensign

Black ball over a black square

For when you want help but are not in distress…

Code flag V indicates 'I require assistance'.

CHAPTER
7

RYA Training Courses
for all ages, abilities and aspirations

Get the most from your time on the water with our range of practical and shorebased courses.

Sail cruising from the beginners' Start Yachting course to Yachtmaster®

Motor cruising from the introductory Helmsman's course to Yachtmaster®

Sailing Away School of Sailing

Graham Snook/MBM

Also, a whole range of navigation and specialist short courses:

> **ESSENTIAL NAVIGATION AND SEAMANSHIP**

> **DAY SKIPPER**

> **COASTAL SKIPPER/ YACHTMASTER® OFFSHORE**

> **YACHTMASTER® OCEAN**

> **DIESEL ENGINE**

> **OFFSHORE SAFETY**

> **VHF RADIO**

> **RADAR**

> **SEA SURVIVAL**

> **FIRST AID**

For further information see www.rya.org.uk, call 00 44 (0)23 8060 4158 for a brochure or email training@rya.org.uk

Distress Alerting equipment guidelines

In view of the increasing number of options for raising the alarm and communicating that a vessel or person is in distress, the RYA issued a new set of Guidelines in the summer of 2010. These recommendations are for pleasure craft under 13.7m in length and are designed to provide pragmatic advice.

Area / Equipment	For craft not more than 3NM from the coast	For craft in GMDSS Sea Area A1 that are more than 3NM from the coast
Portable VHF or portable VHF DSC	Highly recommended where fitting a fixed VHF DSC set is impractical in small day or open boats or similar	Highly recommended where fitting a fixed VHF DSC set is impractical
DSC VHF	Highly recommended	Highly recommended
PLB/EPIRB	Highly recommended that a (406MHz) PLB is attached to an individual in small day or open boats or similar, particularly if only a portable VHF is carried	Highly recommended that a (406MHz) PLB or EPIRB is carried particularly if VHF DSC is not carried
SART/AIS SART	Optional	Optional
Inmarsat or MF/HF radio transceiver with DSC	Not required	Not required
Mobile Phone	Not to be relied upon – last resort	Not to be relied upon – last resort
Battery-operated laser flares	Optional	Optional
Parachute flares	4 recommended if portable VHF, fixed VHF DSC or PLB/EPIRB not carried	4 recommended if VHF DSC or PLB/EPIRB not carried
Red handheld flares	3 unless a reliable alternative day/night locating method is carried	3 unless a reliable alternative day/night locating method is carried
Smoke signals handheld and buoyant	Highly recommended for day boating where no other locating device is carried	Highly recommended for day boating where no other locating device is carried
Day/night flares and mini signal personal survival flares	Recommended as an alternative where space might be at a premium such as for windsurfing	Optional
Luminous dye marker	Optional	Optional

Notes: 1 = Handheld flares provide one minute of smoke. Buoyant flares provide a minimum of 3 minutes of orange smoke.

Compiled by the RYA, and endorsed by the RNLI and MCA, the list outlines the combinations of equipment including flares, EPIRB and VHF DSC, you should consider carrying and using to indicate that you need assistance, depending upon the type of your vessel and where you use it.

For craft sailing outside of Sea Area A1	Comments
Optional – it is assumed that a vessel sailing outside of Sea Area A1 is fitted with communication equipment suitable for the area of operation	A waterproof set is recommended
Highly recommended – note that Sea Area A1 is the boundary for nominal VHF range although in practice sets might work well beyond that.	Highly recommended that 1. DSC VHF is interfaced with GPS for position information and 2. an emergency antenna is carried in case of dismasting.
Highly recommended to carry a (406MHz) PLB or EPIRB since VHF DSC may not work outside Sea Area A1	PLBs are highly recommended for small open boats, dinghies or similar. PLB/EPIRB should be fitted with GPS and 121.5MHz homer built in.
Optional	SART AIS is useful for locating crew members who go overboard where AIS is carried
Inmarsat or marine radio capable of receiving/transmitting and operating in the area of operation	
Not to be relied upon – last resort	Keep dry and charged at all times. **DO NOT RELY ON AS YOUR ONLY MEANS OF COMMUNICATION**
Optional	Recommended if carriage of pyrotechnics is not wanted. Devices still require trial for effectiveness by SAR Services and may in due course negate requirement for flares for location
4 recommended if VHF DSC or PLB/EPIRB not carried	EPIRB/DSC is now the accepted modern method for alerting
3 unless a reliable alternative day/night locating method is carried	These are valuable for 'final mile' locating by day and by night and in poor visibility
Optional for daylight locating. It is assumed that vessels sailing outside area A1 are equipped with a range of locating devices	Valuable for 'final mile' locating in daylight and in reasonable visibility. Contain no explosives. Must burn for a minimum of 3 minutes.[1]
Optional	These are particularly useful as personal distress flares
Optional	Requires testing and then will only be useful as an alternative by day to orange smoke [2]

Also useful for identifying casualty when several vessels are in the same vicinity. 2 = Only really useful for detection from the air.

Air-to-surface direction signals

Sequence of three manoeuvres 'Go in this direction'. May be used to show which way to go to assist another vessel or to indicate direction to a safe haven.

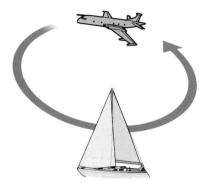

1. Plane circles vessel at least once

2. Plane crosses low, ahead of boat, rocking wings

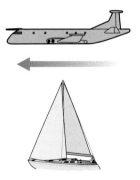

3. Plane flies over boat in the direction to go

Your assistance is no longer required

Shore-to-ship signals

Safe to land here
Vertical waving of arms. white flag, light or flare
Morse code letter K – dah dit dah ▬ ● ▬

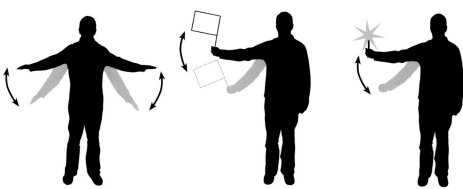

Landing here is dangerous with additional signals that indicate direction of safe landing place

Go this way

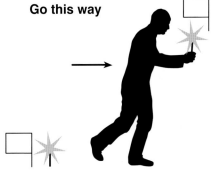

Horizontal waving of arms. white flag, light or flare

Putting one flare on ground and moving in direction of safer landing area with the other indicating direction of safer landing

May also be shown by Morse code light or sound

S – ● ● ●   = landing here is dangerous

R – ● ▬ ●   = land to the right of your current heading

L – ● ▬ ● ●   = land to the left of your current heading

Air-to-surface replies

Message understood

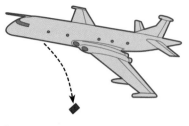

Drop a message   or rocking wings

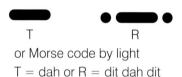

T   R

or Morse code by light

or flashing landing lights on and off twice   T = dah or R = dit dah dit

---

Message not understood

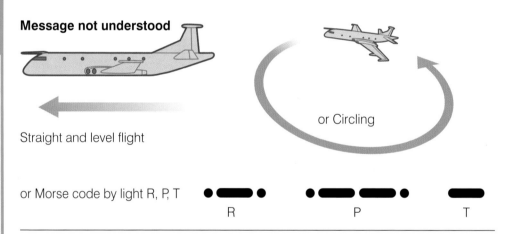

Straight and level flight

or Circling

or Morse code by light R, P, T

R   P   T

Surface-to-air replies

Message understood – I will comply
Change course to required direction
Or Morse code by light T =　●━━　or code and answering pendant

I am unable to comply
Morse code by light N =　━━ ●　or code flag N

Signals used to communicate with vessels in distress

These signals are used by ships, aircraft or persons in distress to communicate with rescue service stations, lifeboats, vessels and aircraft engaged in search-and-rescue operations. Use the most suitable signal for the situation and taking into account the prevailing conditions.

Search-and-rescue unit replies

These indicate that you have been seen and assistance will be given as soon as possible.

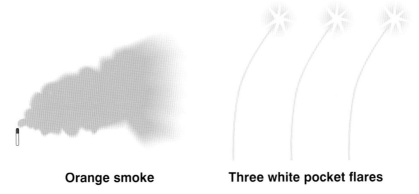

Orange smoke   **Three white pocket flares**

Surface-to-air signals

These are shown by means of lights or flags or by laying out the symbol on the ground or deck in highly contrasting colours.

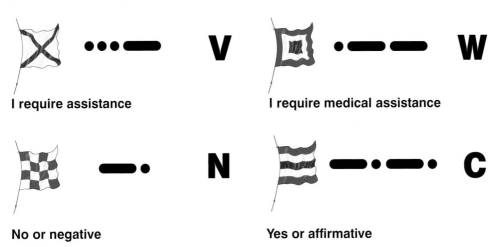

I require assistance   **I require medical assistance**

No or negative   **Yes or affirmative**

Chapter 8 Liferafts

Liferafts are designed to provide the boat's crew with shelter for a limited period should the boat sink or catch fire.

The quality of liferafts varies enormously. Some products marked as a liferaft may be no more than a couple of gas inflated cushions; others provide an acceptable, stable, sheltered environment.

Rafts deteriorate with age and need to be regularly serviced. Always look inside the canister or valise when buying a secondhand raft. Any raft over 12 years old will need to be carefully inspected. Many service agents will not pass a raft fit for service at this age.

Do you need a liferaft?

It is advisable for boats travelling more than 3 miles offshore to carry some form of raft. Boats 13.7m (45ft) in length and over are required under Class XII regulations (see page 16) when at sea to carry a liferaft(s). Even though smaller boats are not required to carry a liferaft, the regulations provide a useful guide for the small-boat owner. The quality of raft to be carried will depend on how far offshore the boat will travel.

Which size liferaft?

The capacity of the liferaft/s should be sufficient to carry all persons on board.

However, if regularly sailing shorthanded, it may be advisable to obtain two smaller rafts instead of one large raft, with the added advantage that the smaller rafts will be lighter and easier to handle. This is because in addition to the ballast pockets, a liferaft uses the weight of its crew to keep it stable in waves, i.e. a boat that can carry eight people but regularly sailed by a crew of two or four would have two four-person rafts instead of one eight-person raft.

Low-cost leisure rafts

There are a number of low cost yacht liferafts that do not meet any prescribed standards. They offer value for money but the quality of construction and standard of their equipment pack can often be insufficient for use offshore.

They are not approved for any commercial operation, yachts sailing under racing rules or Class XII craft. In tests, some lower price rafts have proven to be unreliable – not inflating properly or even at all. On the plus side, they are usually light in weight, which makes them easier to launch.

If limited by budget they are at least better than nothing but if you can afford more then it is better to opt for a raft built to a recognised standard.

Liferaft standards

ISO 9650 Small Craft – Inflatable Liferafts

Introduced by the International Standards Organisation during 2005, ISO 9650 is now recognised as the appropriate standard for leisure boat liferafts.

The standard comprises three parts…

Part 1: Type 1 - Liferafts for offshore use. Subdivided into Group A rafts designed to inflate between –15 to +65 degrees C and Group B rafts that will inflate between 0 and +65 degrees C (air temperature).

Part 2: Type 2 - Liferafts for inshore use. All Part 2 rafts are expected to inflate between 0 and +65 degrees C.

Part 3: Material to be used in liferaft manufacture

The main differences between Part 1: Type 1 and Part 2: Type 2 rafts are shown in the table. Type 2 rafts are, size for size, slightly smaller than Type 1 rafts. Type 1 rafts are more robust than Type 2 rafts.

Type 1 Group A liferafts are recommended for offshore North European waters. Type 2 rafts are considered suitable for inshore waters.

	ISO 9650 Part 1: Type 1	ISO 9650 Part 2: Type 2
Maximum Capacities	4 person to 12 person	4 person to 10 person
Painter length	9 metres	6 metres
Withstand drop of	6 metres	4 metres
Minimum Freeboard	4 person = 250mm	4 person = 200mm
	6 person+ = 300mm	6 person+ = 250mm
Floor	Grp A rafts include thermal floor	Optional

SOLAS, ISO 9650, ISAF specify that the liferaft's main buoyancy is divided into two separate chambers. Each chamber must have sufficient buoyancy to support the maximum capacity of the raft. The chambers must be able to be topped up with a bellows and have pressure relief valves. Each standard also specifies that the liferaft must have a self-erecting canopy. Thermal floors can either be inflatable or a separate 'carpet' of reflective material.

Liferafts built to ISO 9650 Part 1: Type 1 are given a choice of two equipment packs depending on expected duration at sea – less than 24 hours and more than 24 hours. See Liferaft packs on page 110.

The ISAF liferaft is equivalent to an ISO standard one.

SOLAS

Designed for commercial vessels, and required for use on boats 13.7m (45ft) and over travelling 150 miles or more offshore, SOLAS rafts are made and tested to high standards and extremes of operating temperatures.

SOLAS rafts are designed to withstand exposure for 30 days afloat (c/w 20 days for ISO/ISAF), withstand stowage in temperatures from –30 to +60 degrees C, withstand a drop from 18 metres, persons jumping repeatedly into them from 4.5 metres.

SOLAS rafts have lined canopies to provide insulation. Consequently, they are about 30% heavier, tougher and significantly more expensive than ISAF or ISO rafts. The standard covers rafts from 6-person capacity upwards.

A SOLAS rated liferaft

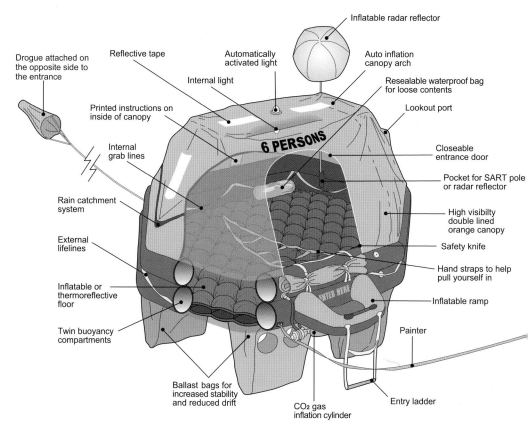

ISAF

Following the 1998 Sydney–Hobart race, the International Sailing Federation developed a specification for liferafts similar to the ISO standard as an interim measure while the new ISO standard was being completed. Since the ISO standard came into force, many manufacturers have adapted their ISAF rafts and rebranded them as ISO rafts. The ISAF specification came into force on 1st January 2003 and covers rafts of maximum capacities of 4 to 12 persons.

ORC

Now superseded by ISAF and ISO specification rafts, ORC (Offshore Racing Congress) liferafts are no longer considered suitable for commercial craft or offshore racing yachts. However, ORC rafts are still offered by some manufacturers for cruising boats. ORC is also known as ISAF part I.

Active Survival Craft

Many yachtsmen planning to go further offshore prefer to carry an active survival craft – a small dinghy adapted to withstand offshore conditions. Accepting that rescue may not be forthcoming, they prefer a craft that gives them the opportunity for self rescue.

Some offshore racing associations approve some makes of active survival craft as an alternative to a liferaft. However, most national authorities do not accept them since there is no recognised standard for active survival craft.

Many are based on an inflatable dinghy fitted with a liferaft gas inflation system and a canopy for shelter. While the crafts can be rowed or sailed to safety, the lack of ballast pockets will make them unstable in a seaway.

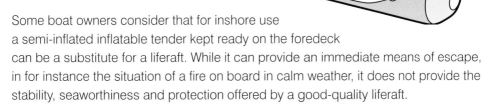

Some boat owners consider that for inshore use a semi-inflated inflatable tender kept ready on the foredeck can be a substitute for a liferaft. While it can provide an immediate means of escape, in for instance the situation of a fire on board in calm weather, it does not provide the stability, seaworthiness and protection offered by a good-quality liferaft.

Canister versus Valise

Liferafts are supplied in either a plastic/glassfibre box or in a fabric valise.
To protect from water damage, most rafts – canister and valise – are vacuum-packed in large polythene bags that rip open when the raft inflates.

Canister

The canister is usually made from two parts held together with straps and provides a hard case to protect the raft from knocks and sharp objects. The canister is not waterproof but the packaging inside should prevent ingress of water.

Pros

■ Easily accessible – often mounted on the coachroof, transom or pushpit
■ Contents protected from physical damage
■ Can self launch when fitted with a Hydrostatic Release Unit (HRU)

Cons

■ More likely to be stolen or washed overboard
■ More expensive to buy
■ Prone to damage from the elements.

Valise rafts

Need to be stowed in a weatherproof locker. A valise should not be left strapped on an exposed deck or buried deep in a locker under piles of sails, fenders or warps.

Pros

■ Cheaper to buy
■ Easier to move due to handles and lighter weight than a rigid canister
■ Less likely to be washed overboard

Cons

■ Likely to be damaged by rough handling – do not throw on to pontoons
■ Harder (and slower) to deploy because it has to be lifted out of a locker
■ Cannot be automatically deployed
■ Cannot be left in an exposed position.

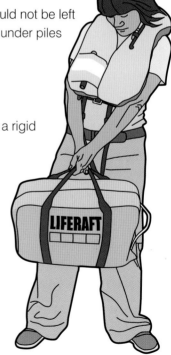

CHAPTER
8

Maintenance

A liferaft must be serviced at the required periods by a competent service agent. Most modern rafts are vacuum packed in large plastic bags. This will usually increase the service period to three years. However, there are many rafts that need to be serviced annually. It's well worth while going along while the raft is being serviced to see it inflated and the quality and amount of equipment packed with the raft.

Hiring

Liferafts can be rented for as a little as a week through to a whole season or more. This may be particularly useful for those that sail shorthanded with one raft for most of the year and only occasionally with a full crew where two rafts would be needed.

Hydrostatic release units (HRUs)

HRUs are designed to automatically release a liferaft when the boat sinks to a depth between 1 to 4 metres (3 to 13 feet). While HRUs are required on liferafts on commercial boats, it's an optional fit for leisure craft.

The HRU cuts the securing strap holding the raft in place allowing it to float to the surface while the painter remains attached to a weak link on the HRU.

As the boat sinks further, it tugs on the painter to trigger the liferaft's inflation system. The buoyancy of the inflated raft causes the weak link to break and release the raft from the boat.

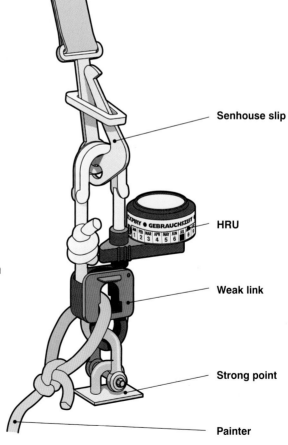

Senhouse slip

HRU

Weak link

Strong point

Painter

Liferaft packs

Generally, the contents of a liferaft will depend on the type of raft – leisure, ISAF, ISO 9650 or SOLAS. The minimum contents required under each specification are listed opposite. Note that ISO 9650 Part 1 Type 1 rafts have a choice of packs suitable for survival for less than 24 hours or more than 24 hours. You specify which pack when you purchase or service the liferaft.

The standard pack can be supplemented with extra equipment as long as it can fit! Ask your service agent. If not, add it to your Grab Bag. Carefully consider what you may need for the area you will be sailing.

Find out what you have in your liferaft before you need it!

Many items inside the raft will have a limited life – flares, water, food etc – that need to be replaced when the raft is serviced. When possible, check the quality of equipment in your raft – cheap rafts may have poor quality equipment.

Grab Bag

Designed to supplement the contents of the liferaft, the grab bag must be watertight and able to float. Stow the contents of the bag in separate waterproof containers that can be opened with cold wet fingers. The containers themselves may also prove useful for collecting and using rain water for drinking or for stowing opened food.

Some sailing yacht racing rules specify what you must have in the grab bag. Check them!

Most boat owners will find that some items cannot be stowed since they are required for everyday use. In which case, make up a laminated 'grab bag list' of what to take with you. Stow grab bag extras where you know you will find them. Use the boat equipment plan as your guide.

The illustrations on the following pages suggest a range of items but what you put in is up to you.

Item	SOLAS A	SOLAS B	ISO 9650 24 hours or more	ISO 9650 less than 24 hours	ISAF	ORC	Typical leisure raft (D-pack)
Buoyant knife	1	1	1	1	1	1	1
Bailer	1	1	1	1	1	1	1
Sponges	2	2	2	2	1pp	2	2
Paddles	2	2	2	2	2	2	2
Whistle	1	1	1	1	1	1	–
Torches	1	1	1	1	2	1	–
Heliograph	1	1	1	1	1	–	–
Anti seasick pills	6pp	6pp	6pp	6pp	6pp	–	–
Seasick bag	1pp	1pp	1pp	1pp	1pp	–	–
Red h/h flares	6	3	6	3	3	3	–
Para rocket flares	4	2	2	2	Grab bag	–	–
Buoyant smoke flare	2	1	–	–	–	–	–
TPA	2	2	2	–	2	–	–
Repair kit	1	1	1	1	1	1	1
Water	0.5lt pp	–	1.5lt pp	–	Grab bag	–	–
Food	10,000kJ pp	–	10,000kJ pp	–	Grab bag	–	–
First aid kit	1	1	1	–	1	–	–
Bellows	1	1	1	1	1	1	1
Throwing line – 30m	1	1	1	1	1	–	1
Drogue	2	2	1	1	2	1	1
Waterproof notebook	–	–	–	–	1	–	–
Signal card	1	1	–	–	–	1	1
Sea survival instructions	–	–	–	–	1	–	–
Leak stoppers	Set	Set	–	–	Set	Set	–
Radar reflector	1	1	–	–	–	–	–
Fishing kit	1	–	–	–	–	–	–
Tin opener	3	–	–	–	–	–	–
Graduated drinking cup	1	–	–	–	–	–	–

pp = per person

Extra kit to take with you into the liferaft

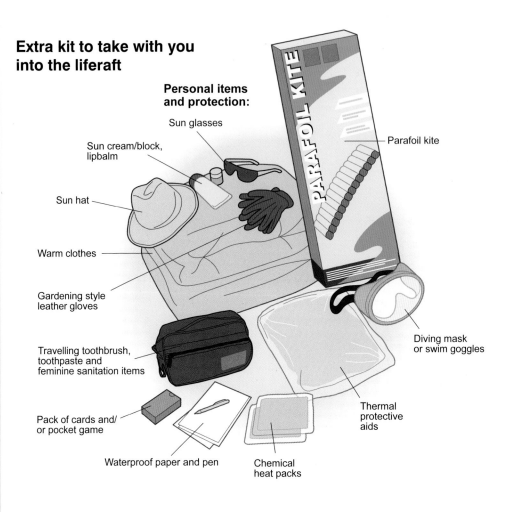

Personal items and protection:

Sun glasses

Sun cream/block, lipbalm

Parafoil kite

Sun hat

Warm clothes

Gardening style leather gloves

Travelling toothbrush, toothpaste and feminine sanitation items

Diving mask or swim goggles

Pack of cards and/ or pocket game

Thermal protective aids

Waterproof paper and pen

Chemical heat packs

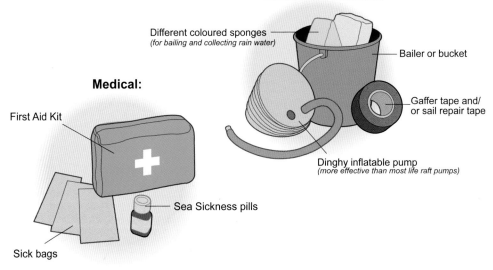

Liferaft maintenance:

Different coloured sponges
(for bailing and collecting rain water)

Bailer or bucket

Medical:

First Aid Kit

Gaffer tape and/ or sail repair tape

Dinghy inflatable pump
(more effective than most life raft pumps)

Sea Sickness pills

Sick bags

Survival and maintenance items:

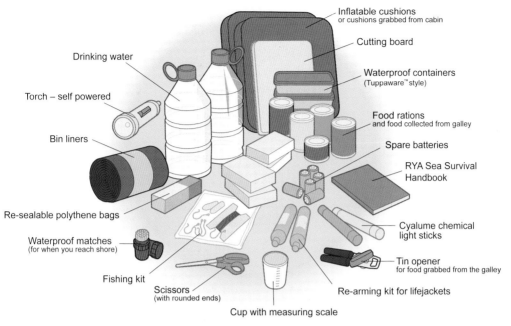

Inflatable cushions
or cushions grabbed from cabin

Cutting board

Drinking water

Waterproof containers
(Tuppaware™ style)

Torch – self powered

Food rations
and food collected from galley

Bin liners

Spare batteries

RYA Sea Survival
Handbook

Re-sealable polythene bags

Cyalume chemical
light sticks

Waterproof matches
(for when you reach shore)

Tin opener
for food grabbed from the galley

Fishing kit

Scissors
(with rounded ends)

Re-arming kit for lifejackets

Cup with measuring scale

Rescue and navigation:

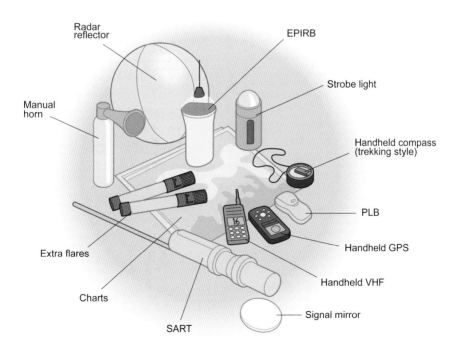

Radar
reflector

EPIRB

Strobe light

Manual
horn

Handheld compass
(trekking style)

PLB

Extra flares

Handheld GPS

Handheld VHF

Charts

Signal mirror

SART

If rescued by helicopter, you will not be able to take a large case with you! But you will need some basics after you've been dropped off ashore. It's worthwhile, therefore, to pack a small waterproof bag with all the crew's essentials (such as money, credit cards, spare spectacles, personal medication, the boat's papers, passports, house and car keys etc.) together. Losing your boat is bad enough but sleeping rough, not being able to buy a train, plane or ferry ticket home and then having to break into your car and house will make it worse!

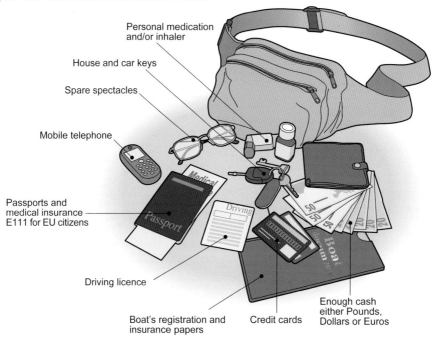

Personal medication and/or inhaler

House and car keys

Spare spectacles

Mobile telephone

Passports and medical insurance E111 for EU citizens

Driving licence

Boat's registration and insurance papers

Credit cards

Enough cash either Pounds, Dollars or Euros

ISAF Offshore Special Regulations recommendations for Grab Bag contents

As part of the Offshore Special regulations for sailing yachts taking part in races, the International Sailing Federation requires specific safety-related equipment to be carried on board each vessel involved in the event. Ideally this equipment will be stored in one or more watertight grab bags with in-built buoyancy. These bags should be stored in an accessible location where they can be easily reached in the event of an emergency. These requirements are updated on a regular basis and the current requirements can be found at http://www.sailing.org/specialregulations.php.

The bag should have inherent flotation, a lanyard and clip, be marked with the boat's name and have an area of at least $0.1m^2$ of fluorescent orange colour on the outside.

Chapter 9 Dealing with Fire

Boats burn easily and fire onboard can have devastating effects and will often require abandoning ship – especially on boats that carry petrol or liquid petroleum gas (LPG – butane and propane).

Petrol vapour and LPG is heavier than air. Escaped gas will accumulate in the boat's bilges and can form an explosive mixture with air.

Turn off supply to gas appliances as close to the source as possible – preferably at the bottle – when not required. Ensure all crew know gas routine.

As always, prevention is better than cure so simple precautions should be followed…

- Fit and maintain portable fire extinguishers

- Fit automatic extinguisher in engine compartment

- Turn engine off when refuelling

- Don't overfill tanks – especially outboard engine petrol tanks

- Make sure fuel tank caps are properly secured

- Ventilate the engine compartment after fuelling and before starting engine. This is particularly important for petrol installations

- Avoid fuel spillage and clean any spillage that does occur immediately – dispose of cloths carefully

- Limit the number of fuel cans aboard – stow in properly ventilated lockers whenever possible

- Fit an approved gas and vapour detector

- Fit smoke alarm

- Keep engine bay and electrics clean and tidy

- Install correct size wiring

- Make sure smokers are aware of the need for extra care – preferably do not smoke below decks.

Make a plan

Formulate a plan of what to do in the event of fire. Brief crew about the plan, point out the position of fire extinguishers, liferaft and grab bag and who to call. Crew should move as far away as possible on deck from fire.

Being trapped in the accommodation is the most immediate danger therefore the best place to fit fire extinguishers is at exits – exit from forward cabin, exit from after cabin and exit from guest cabins, exit of main cabin – so that you can knock down flames and exit to deck. When fighting fire, always ensure you have a clear escape route.

Fire triangle

A fire needs fuel, heat and air to burn. Permanently remove just one part and the fire will go out.

Fire extinguishers

All extinguishers made to BS EN 3 are red with a colour-coded area to show the type of extinguishant.

They are rated by the types and size of fire for which they are suitable.

A – carbonaceous (wood, glassfibre, upholstery)
B – flammable liquids (petrol, diesel)
C – flammable gases (butane, propane)

An extinguisher will be rated with a number and letter rating – for example 5A/34B or 13A/113B. The larger the number, the bigger the fire of that type the extinguisher can tackle. For each type of fire there are specified test conditions for each level of extinguishing power. The number given in the fire rating links to the size of fire it is classified as being suitable for. For example, a type B fire extinguisher is required to extinguish the specified volume of liquid indicated e.g. 21B refers to test conditions using 21 litres of the specified fuel.

Most fire extinguishers can cope with two types of fire and some will deal with three.

Although seen on most boats, dry powder is not ideal for accommodation areas because the extinguishant will cause breathing difficulties and may even reduce visibility. It's messy and if not cleaned up quickly it will corrode metals. However, it is the most effective extinguishant available. Use manual extinguishers to knock down flames then leave the cabin and fight fire through the companionway door.

Under Class XII regulations, boats over 13.7m are required in the UK to fit minimum fire fighting equipment – see page 18.

Service or replace extinguishers at prescribed date. Most extinguishers have a five-year service life. Many do not print their date of manufacture on the extinguisher so it's a good idea to note it on purchase in the boat's logbook.

Regularly shake dry powder extinguishers to prevent powder coagulating.

Extinguishants

Water (A) – extinguishers painted red with no zone of other colour – alternatively, there is plenty of it around (the sea) to be picked up in a bucket (tie lanyard to bucket). Water fire extinguishers are available but are relatively large and heavy. Cools fire. Do not use on liquid, gas, electrical or cooking fat fires.

Dry powder (ABC) – extinguishers red with a zone of blue – use on solids, flammable liquid (petrol/diesel engine fires) but not cooking oil. Do not use on a gas fire without isolating the gas supply first, otherwise there may be an explosion. Messy but very effective at knocking down flames. Not hazardous to health if a small quantity is inhaled but avoid using in enclosed spaces.

AFFF foam (AB) – extinguishers red with a cream zone – use on solids, flammable liquid (petrol/diesel engine fires) but not cooking oil, gas and electrical fires.

Carbon dioxide (CO2) (B) – extinguishers red with a black zone – used in manual and automatic extinguishers but not often found on boats. Use on flammable liquid fires but not cooking oil fires. Do not use on people – expanding gas is cold and can give severe cold burns. Do not use in confined spaces.

Automatic extinguishers for engine compartments

Use single extinguisher of the correct size for the compartment – two separate extinguishers are likely to fire independently and will not have sufficient capacity on their own to kill the fire.

Most extinguishers can be triggered either automatically when fire detected or remotely by cable or electrical operation. If possible, close off or cover air vents to engine compartment to minimise air supply.

CHAPTER
9

Automatic extinguisher extinguishants

Due to the location, a number of different extinguishants can be used in an engine compartment.

Halocarbon gas – a number of environmentally-friendly gas extinguishants are available (FM 200, FE 36) for engine compartments. They are clean and will not damage the engine.

Micro-powders – fine powder extinguishant – sometimes called an aerosol (not to be confused with household aerosols) – is created from a solid material and therefore no propellant gas to escape. It works by chemically reacting with fire. Has a long life – 15 years – compared to halocarbon gas extinguishers.

Dry powder (ABC) – similar to manual extinguisher. Can be used in naturally aspirated engine compartments. Dry powder will damage engines with turbo or super chargers, is messy and corrosive.

Fire blanket

Traditionally used to smother flames on liquid (cooking oil) or people they also make a good protective shield when passing close to a fire. Fit the blanket on the side of the galley away from companionway so that it can pulled out and used for escape. Hold the blanket with the handles turned inside.

Gas on board

To meet safety and insurance requirements, the gas systems on boats used for non-commercial leisure purposes should meet BS5482:3 if built before August 2000 and ISO 10239 standards if built after that date. Details about installing gas on board a boat are extensive.

It's recommended that any work on the gas system is undertaken by a qualified gas engineer.

If the boat is to be used on the British Waterways then it will also have to pass the BSS scheme inspection – see page 19.

A qualified gas engineer specialising in boat installations will be able to give a detailed report on your boat's gas installation and provide a Gas Safety Inspection Record for your insurers.

There are, however, some parts of the system that need to be checked on a regular basis.

■ Gas appliances should be serviced annually to ensure they remain in a safe and efficient condition and replaced if any deterioration is found.

■ Flexible hose must be to ISO2928:2003 and replaced every five years or if they are showing signs of leaks, flaws, damage or bleaching. The date of manufacture is shown on the hose.

■ Regulators should be replaced if more than 10 years old.

■ Regulators should be the correct type for the gas being used – butane or propane.

■ Gas bottles should be stowed in a dedicated and properly ventilated gas locker.

■ Gas appliances should be fitted with flame-failure devices.

CHAPTER
9

Gas detectors

Electronic gas detectors can be fitted to warn of excessive LPG levels in the bilge. The sensors need to be mounted in as low a position as possible but higher than the level of bilge water. Do not mount sensors under gas appliances where they can be triggered by small amounts of escaped gas.

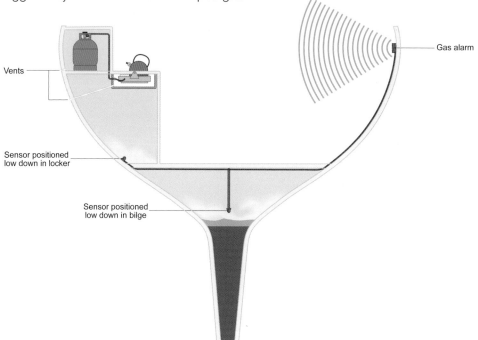

Vents

Gas alarm

Sensor positioned low down in locker

Sensor positioned low down in bilge

Gas levels are considered to be dangerous when they reach the 100% Lower Explosive Level (LEL). Most gas detectors are calibrated to sound the alarm when the gas levels reach 10% of the LEL. Gas can be smelt when the concentration is less than 1% LEL due to a strong smelling chemical added to the gas by the suppliers.

Carbon Monoxide detectors

Boats built after June 1998 should have been fitted with room sealed gas appliances – apart from cookers – to prevent the escape of carbon monoxide (CO).

Known as the silent killer, CO is an odourless, tasteless, colourless, non-irritating gas that is poisonous to human beings. It is created when there is insufficient oxygen provided to a burning flame. The early symptoms of CO poisoning are drowsiness, nausea, dizziness and headaches and poor decision making.

Always ensure that cabins are well ventilated, even on cold wet days, when using naked-flame appliances.

Fit a CO detector at around head height.

Chapter 10 Before you go out

The Boy Scouts' motto of 'be prepared' could equally apply to those who go afloat.

You'll need to ask yourself some questions and take some actions before you go. Remember it's not only a requirement of SOLAS V to be properly prepared but it's also common sense! If the conditions are not right, don't go.

Who knows where you are going?

Tell a responsible person ashore where you are going, what time you will be back, how many people are on board and what to do if you don't return at the specified time (see page 154 – CG 66). Let them know if you're going to be late.

On longer passages, file a passage plan with the Coastguard. Tell them if you change the plan. Call them when you complete the passage. Note: the Coastguard won't initiate a search if you don't contact them. On the other hand, if your contact ashore raises the alarm the Coastguard will know exactly where to start looking for you.

Weather and tides

Is your boat suitable for the conditions? Will your crew be able to cope with the expected conditions? How's the tide going to affect your passage plan? What ports will you be able to enter, taking into account the wind direction and the state of the tide? And how does that fit in with your contingency plan? What will the conditions be around headlands and through tidal races? Will you be able to get back?

Engine and fuel

Has your engine been regularly serviced? Is it running smoothly? Have you completed your engine checks? Do you have sufficient spares on board? Do you have sufficient fuel on board? Boats are fuel thirsty – it's not unusual for a motorboat to have fuel consumption figures as great as one mile per gallon. At most, consumption is often only 6–12mpg – even in 'economical' displacement boats.

Carry sufficient fuel to allow a third of your capacity to get to your destination, a third to get back and a third spare – a boat's consumption increases in heavy weather and against a foul tide.

Communication

For coastal waters a VHF radio is essential. A mobile phone is a poor substitute and should not be relied upon as your only means of communication while at sea. Vessels should also be equipped with a suitable combination of EPIRB/PLB, DSC VHF and flares. This is discussed in detail on page 80.

Personal flotation devices

The decision about wearing personal buoyancy is often based upon factors such as weather conditions and the experience of the crew. Making these judgements is often not that easy. Therefore, in order to help clarify when a lifejacket or personal buoyancy aid needs to be worn, the RYA recommends that you wear a lifejacket or buoyancy aid unless you are sure you don't need to based upon your assessment of the specific situation. Personal buoyancy should be appropriate to the type of boat and boating you are doing. This is discussed in more detail on page 24.

Training

Are your and your crew's skills good enough for the planned passage? If not you should be asking yourself, should you really be out on the water until you have had the right training and are confident in your ability.

Safety brief

As skipper you should ensure that everyone on board knows where the safety equipment is stowed and how to use it. Talk them through your passage and pilotage plan as well as your contingency plans should something go wrong.

Don't forget the less obvious safety equipment i.e. how to drop anchor or how to read your current position off the GPS or chart.

Are your crew familiar with boating? Is there anything you should know about them? Can they swim? Do they have medical problems that you need to be aware of such as asthma, diabetes or angina for example? As skipper, their safety is your responsibility.

Safety brief checklist

- ☐ **Lifejackets** – check condition, lights, when and how to don

- ☐ **Harnesses** – when and where to clip on

- ☐ **Flares** – where stowed and how to fire

- ☐ **Liferaft** – where stowed and how to launch

- ☐ **Grab Bag** – where it is, other items (such as water, food etc)

- ☐ **On board hazards** – boom, winches, cleats, ropes etc

- ☐ **Anchoring procedure**

- ☐ **How to start engine**

- ☐ **Lifebuoy/Dan buoy**

- ☐ **VHF radio** – Mayday and DSC procedures

- ☐ **GPS** – how to read off position

- ☐ **Bilge pump** – where and how to use it

- ☐ **First Aid kit** – where

- ☐ **Fire extinguishers** – where, what type and how to use them

- ☐ **Medicines** – are they taking any, sea sick tablets (asthma, diabetes, heart?)

- ☐ **Clothing** – spare clothing, suncream

- ☐ **Lookout** – tell me what you see, I may not have seen it!

- ☐ **Passage Plan** – where we are going, contingency plans

- ☐ **MOB recovery equipment** – where and how to use

- ☐ **Watch rota** – when to call skipper?

- ☐ **Can they swim?**

- ☐ **Medical problems?**

Where is it?

Since safety equipment is often stowed out of sight, it makes good sense to make a basic plan showing where the gear is stowed. Show it to the crew and pin it up where they will see it. Some skippers place a copy on the back of the heads' door, where crew will have the time to contemplate it!

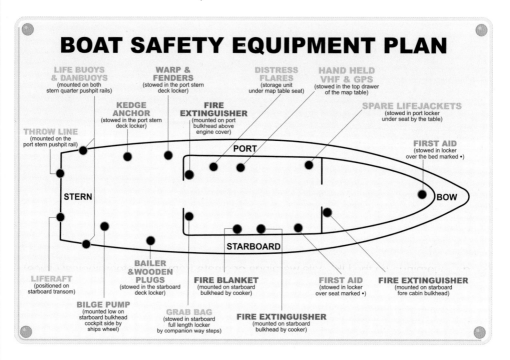

Navtex

Weather information is essential to ensure a safe passage. While ashore weather forecasts can be obtained from numerous sources but out at sea specific equipment will be needed.

Navtex is an international system specified by the International Maritime Organisation as part of the GMDSS for broadcasting Marine Safety Information in a text format. It requires either a dedicated receiver or an active antenna coupled to a computer that can receive 518kHz and/or 490kHz transmissions. The receiver should be left switched on ready to receive transmissions. Most dedicated receivers have to be switched between one frequency and the other but a few can receive both frequencies simultaneously.

All Navtex messages transmitted on 518kHz, no matter where they originated in the World, are broadcast in English. In the UK, 518kHz transmissions include the Shipping forecast. Transmissions on 490kHz are usually in the local language. In the UK, 490kHz transmissions include the Inshore waters forecast and coastal station reports.

Navtex is designed to work out at sea beyond the safe water buoy. It works on medium frequency (MF) and has a minimum range of 270 miles, but can be greater than this. Because the range of the MF signal is affected by atmospheric conditions, it is important to ensure that your Navtex receiver is tuned to receive signals for the area you are in and the one you are sailing to, otherwise the receiver may not be able to sync with the transmission.

Navtex messages are prefixed by a 4-character group that denotes the identity of the transmitting station, the message category and its serial number.

The GMDSS divides the World into 16 Navareas plus the polar regions. Each Navarea has up to 24 stations. The UK is in Navarea 1. Since the system is only working on two frequencies, to avoid over transmission, the broadcasts are transmitted in 10 minute time slots at specific times on a four-hourly schedule (similar to the system used for VHF MSI broadcasts transmitted by the Maritime & Coastguard Agency and Maritime Rescue Co-ordination Centres).

Most sets allow you to filter out certain categories of messages but the category code 00 denotes urgent traffic and will always be shown. Messages that are always shown are A, B, C or E.

Navigational categories are…

A – navigational warnings (in the UK, navigational warnings originate from the Hydrographic Office)

B – gale warnings (in the UK, gale warnings originate from the Meteorological Office)

C – ice reports

D – distress alerting plus SAR/piracy information

E – weather forecasts (in the UK, weather forecasts originate from the Meteorological Office)

F – pilot services information

J – satellite navigation messages

K – other navigational messages

L – drilling rig movements

V – amplification of navigational warnings in A on 490kHz

W – subfacts/gunfacts (brief details of submarine exercises and gunnery range firings including VHF channels and broadcast times)

Z – no message in hand

■ G, H, I – are designated for Decca, Loran and Omega navigational system messages.

The UK coastal radio stations are Niton (ID: E 518kHz and I and T (French service) on 490kHz), Cullercoats (ID: G on 518 and U on 490) and Portpatrick (ID: O on 518 and C on 490). A full list of broadcast stations, their location and transmission schedule can be found in a number of publications. See MGN 375 at http://www.dft.gov.uk/mca/mcga-mnotice.htm?textobjid=633053BA153B9EE3 for further information.

VHF

Maritime safety information, which includes both weather information and navigational warnings, is broadcast on VHF by the Coastguard Maritime Rescue Co-ordination Centres (MRCC) every three hours. The schedule is published in a number of places including the RYA website at http://www.rya.org.uk/weathertides/go/msi.

Longwave/ medium wave radio receiver

The Shipping Forecast is broadcast on the BBC Radio 4 long wave at 0048 (also FM), 0520, 1201, 0520 (also FM) and 1754. To receive it, you will need a radio capable of receiving 198 KHz long wave. The bulletins include a gale warning summary, general synopsis, sea-area forecasts and coastal station reports. Gale warnings are also broadcast at the first available programme break.

Some bulletins include inshore forecasts 0048 and on BBC Radio 3 at 0535. The inshore forecast covers up to 12 miles offshore up until 1800 the following day.

Inshore forecasts are broadcast on FM by local stations – times vary.

Other methods for obtaining weather forecasts

There are now a number of ways of receiving weather information when at sea. We have already mentioned the weather receiving services provided by Inmarsat – see page 90 – downloadable through Inmarsat C and Mini C transceivers, and the Inmarsat Fleet broadband satellite service. There is also the HF radio services, which can be downloaded on to a laptop computer via a HF receiver see page 84. Some of the other methods are shown here.

Nasa Weatherman Using the radioteletype service broadcast by the German Weather Agency (DWD) on HF, it's a dedicated HF receiver which picks up the free DWD broadcasts, and displays them on a LCD screen. Simple and relatively low cost.

XM and Sirius systems For those cruising in US waters, satellite radio receivers are available that can be connected to a chart plotter to download weather information. It's a subscription service and provides a broad range of weather information from animated synoptic charts to weather radar images, and storm tracking.

Garmin GDL40 cellular phone system Garmin produce a cellular phone antenna that connects to their chart plotters. It downloads weather information using the mobile phone system and is therefore only applicable to coastal sailors. The information downloaded includes weather radar, sea surface temperatures, wind speed and direction, wave height/period and direction and current conditions supplied from meteorological buoys.

Telephone and fax service Marinecall (www.marinecall.co.uk) provide Met Office weather forecast service by telephone for UK waters – inshore and offshore waters and European sailing centres from NE France to Portugal. Calls cost 60p/minute and are accessed by 09068 500 prefix followed by the forecast area code. The forecasts are for 10 days.

SMS weather service for mobile phones Met Marine (www.metmarine.com) offer SMS text weather forecasts for the English Channel coasts. French Mediterranean, French Atlantic, Spanish Mediterranean, Greece and Turkey. The forecasts include wind speed, trend and direction, pressure, visibility, weather, temperature for the day and next 24 hours. It's updated every 6 hours. Tel: 0161 444 8555.

Smartphones, of course provide the whole range of internet weather sites.

Barometer Whether you're unable to receive a forecast or simply wish to confirm the forecast is correct, a barometer will show whether a change is on the way. Rapidly dropping pressure is a warning of strong winds coming.

Echosounder and lead line

While a lead line will give you an accurate measurement of the depth in shallow water, and an indication of the type of seabed, for most yachtsmen an echosounder is the preferred choice. It's immediate and can measure greater depths.

In addition to simply telling you the depth of water, it can also be used, in conjunction with a chart, to navigate along depth contours in poor visibility.

Most echosounders have a shallow water alarm, some also include a deep water alarm.

Variable frequency echosounders give a better response over a broader range of depths. Fishfinders provide a graphical view of the seabed and can show trends more easily.

GPS receivers and chart plotters

The Navstar Global Positioning System is a global satellite navigational system that was developed by the US Department of Defence and is now run by the US Air Force. It's free to use and has a constellation of up to 32 satellites.

The cost of GPS receivers is now so low that every boat can have one or more, powered either from the boat's batteries or independently on dry-cell batteries.

A receiver requires only four satellites – out of the eight or so available at any one time – to calculate a position in latitude and longitude accurate to about 10 metres.

GPS receivers base their position on the World Geodetic System 1984 (WGS84). To plot a position direct on to a chart, the chart must be drawn to the same datum.

While new UKHO (UK Hydrographic Office) charts are now based on WGS 84, older charts were based on the Ordnance Survey of Great Britain 1936 (OSGB36) datum. European charts may be based on European 1950 datum (ED50). Depending on where you are in the UK, there is about 100 metres difference between WGS84 and OSGB36 – enough to make the difference between hitting or missing a patch of rocks! A distance of 100m on a chart of 1:50000 is about 2cm.

GPS positions are often provided to three decimal places of a minute. This can give a perceived accuracy of less than 2 metres. Although charts are accurate, they may not be that accurate in areas that were surveyed decades previously. Allow for a sensible margin of safety particularly when navigating in poor visibility. Confirm position and safety by using other means such as plotting bearings, the echosounder or radar.

It's good practice to note and plot your position regularly and the time it was taken when on passage. The frequency will vary depending on your speed and the proximity of dangers. A yacht travelling at 5 knots on a 100-mile passage in open water need only plot every hour. On fast craft, this needs to be completed more often, every 15 minutes to half an hour. If the GPS fails, either due to an electrical fault or, very occasionally, due to a failure of the GPS system, you then have the information available to start navigating traditionally.

Galileo, the European version of GPS, is scheduled to be operational in 2013 and is intended to be accurate to one metre. Galileo will be compatible with GPS. GLONASS, the Russian system, now supported by India, is fully operational and is compatible with GPS.

Avoid using buoys as waypoints – it has been known for craft under the control of a GPS-led autopilot to crash into buoys. Some buoys are also popular turning marks for others on the same route. Using the same buoys can lead to a GPS-aided collision. Always keep a good lookout.

Chart plotters

Chart plotters, usually with an integral GPS receiver, provide an instant 'where are we now' position. There are two basic types – those based on raster charts and those that use vector charts. Raster charts are scans (direct copies) of paper charts while vector charts are made up of levels of data taken from paper charts.

Whenever planning a route on a chart plotter always zoom in to make sure that all the details have been shown, copy the route on to a paper chart of the best scale possible. It's easy to plot routes on an electronic chart that can take you into danger.

Chart cartridges need to be updated as often as paper charts. The main suppliers offer updating services.

Smartphones offer the choice of downloading apps of charts which can be used alongside the in-built GPS.

Radar

Developed during the Second World War, RAdio Detection And Ranging (RADAR) equipment transmits a pulse of radio frequency from a rotating antenna and then 'listens' for the returning echo. Boat radars use the 9cm X-band frequency. Anything that can reflect the signal sufficiently will be shown on the screen. It requires skill to interpret the returns correctly.

If you have a radar on board and are using it in restricted visibility, you are required under IRPCS (Colregs) Rule 19 to determine if risk of collision exists and, of course, take avoiding action if need be. In other words, if you fit radar you must know how to use it. The RYA administers a one-day radar course. For contact details see page 157.

Automatic Identification System (AIS)

AIS A is used by ships to continually broadcast identification and location details to other vessels and Vessel Traffic Services (VTS). The IMO (International Maritime Organization) requires all ships, except warships, over 300grt and all passenger vessels to transmit their details on AIS. Details are broadcast up to every 10 seconds when under way (every 3 minutes when anchored) on dedicated VHF frequencies.

AIS receivers process the details, list the information and can feed close-to real-time details to a chart plotter and/or radar.

Amongst the information that may be included in the AIS broadcast is the MMSI number, call sign speed and course, making it easier for a small craft to identify a ship.

AIS B transceivers, with built-in GPS sets, can be fitted to recreational and small commercial vessels. They broadcast limited information that can be shown on other vessels' chart plotting and radar displays. However, it should be noted not all ships are fitted with the latest equipment able to display this information. Also, to reduce clutter, it is possible for ships with AIS A to filter out small craft signals. It should be noted that position-reporting information is updated less frequently on AIS B than it is on AIS A, therefore potentially creating a higher level of inaccuracy.

Note that in some countries' territorial waters, it is mandatory for AIS transponders to be carried by all vessels.

Log

Fit a log that can provide distance run as well as speed. Some sports boat speedometers only provide speed. Distance run combined with a course, derived from the compass heading, allows the navigator to estimate the boat's position.

Binoculars

A pair of waterproof 7 x 50 binoculars is the best option for use on boats. The seven times magnification is about as much that can be held steady on a moving vessel. Stabilised binoculars with a higher magnification can be used but they are often heavier and more awkward to handle and hold steady.

The 50mm objective lens combined with the 7x magnification creates a pupil in the ocular lens of just over 7mm. The pupil of a human eye dilates, at most, to about 6 to 7mm diameter, therefore 7 x 50 binoculars are the best for use in low light since they allow the most amount of light into the eye.

If using binoculars when wearing spectacles, roll back the rubber cups on the ocular lenses so that the field of view is at its optimum.

Binoculars with a buit-in compass allow bearings to be taken at the same time.

Compasses

A steering compass is essential on all boats. Combined with a chart and a log, a steering compass provides you the basic equipment with which to navigate your boat safely.

Check the steering compass for deviation caused by ferrous objects or electrical wires passing close to the compass. The compass should be at least 0.5m from possible sources of deviation. Take care not to place magnetic objects close to the compass otherwise you will be given a false heading.

The compass should be at least 0.5m from possible sources of deviation.

A hand bearing compass is used to take bearings of marks, shown on the chart, and allows you to plot your position. There are two different types – those held up to the eye and those held at arm's length.

Some hand bearing compasses can be fitted into a holder and used as a steering compass. When buying, check the compass card settles quickly and holds its position easily. Steering and hand bearing compasses should include some form of lighting so that they can be used at night.

Torch/spotlight

There's a place for several waterproof torches on a cruising boat from small red lights for use at night to mega candlepower searchlights. A powerful spotlight has a variety of uses. It can be used to illuminate unlit buoys and withies when navigating through a harbour; it can be used for signalling; it can be used for searching for a MOB; it can be used for shining on to your boat's sails or superstructure to make yourself more visible to shipping and, if all else fails it can be used to shine directly towards the bridge of a ship to get their attention if they should be on a collision course with you.

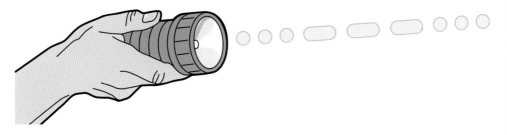

It's bad etiquette to use a spotlight like a car headlight to continuously light the sea ahead or to shine it at other boats since it will dazzle and can temporarily blind and limit the night vision of other seafarers.

Night vision devices

Night vision monoculars or binoculars may be useful if looking in the local area for unlit marks or buoys or a MOB. They work by amplifying the ambient light. Early models of night vision devices use Generation 1 technology and intensify the light up to 20,000 times. Generation 2 models amplify the light up to 75,000 times. Generation 3 technology is limited to the defence and SAR services and is not available to the general public.

At the time of writing, thermal imaging night sights are also being introduced for night navigation. Specifications suggest they may have a greater range.

Charts, nautical almanacs, pilot books and navigation instruments

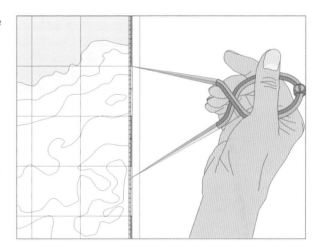

It's important to use up-to-date charts wherever you plan to cruise: new navigation marks are added and existing ones can be repositioned, their light characteristics changed and even their shapes and type.

Admiralty charts, produced by the UK Hydrographic Office (UKHO), and Imray produce charts particularly designed for leisure craft use in several different sizes. Full size admiralty charts, used on ships, are often too large to be easily accommodated aboard a boat. Both organisations produce small craft folios – sets of small size charts – for the popular boating areas. Imray charts are folded and often include harbour plans.

If you use a GPS receiver or electronic chart plotter, ensure your charts are referenced to the WGS84 satellite datum, otherwise you will have to apply a correction to the position provided by the GPS set. Alternatively, alter the GPS set up to provide lat/long converted to your charts' data.

Both UKHO and Imray publish Notices to Mariners which list changes and corrections that can be applied to your charts. Notices to Mariners can be found on www.ukho.gov.uk, while Imray corrections are at www.imray.com.

Nautical almanacs provide information on sailing directions, tidal predictions, local sources of weather information and other important maritime information. This information is vital when coastal or offshore cruising. Sailing directions and pilot books are also essential when cruising off an unfamiliar coast.

Navigational instruments such as a Breton plotter or a parallel ruler, dividers and soft pencils will be needed to use the charts for navigation. Electronic plotters have their place but all skippers must have the skill and ability to navigate using paper charts. Sea schools and adult education programmes run RYA navigational classes. Contact the RYA for details of your nearest establishment.

Under the SOLAS V regulations, a Table of Emergency Signals must be carried aboard the boat. Most almanacs include the table and it is also provided on the back of UKHO Leisure chart folios.

At night, to save the crew's night vision, it is advisable to use red lighting throughout the boat and especially when navigating at the chart table.

Anchors, cables and anchor deck fittings

It is often forgotten that when all else fails, the anchor is the skipper's tool of last resort. It can be the only way of keeping you and your boat either off the rocks or from drifting further offshore.

Yet, sadly, many boats carry undersized anchors. Although not suitable for strong winds they can often be used as the kedge or 'Lunch' anchor.

There are two basic types of anchor – those that dig themselves into the sea bottom such as the CQR, Bruce, Danforth and Delta (and their similar-design competitors) – often known as high-holding power (HHP) anchors – and those designed to hook on to the surface of the sea bed (such as Fisherman's and Grapnel).

Digging anchors provide much greater holding power compared to their weight and are designed to bury themselves into sand, mud, clay and gravel bottoms.

The different designs have their advantages and disadvantages and there are numerous magazine articles that rate the anchors. However, much appears to depend on the type and consistency of the sea bed and how well the anchor was set. It's hard to find repeatable test data. With that said, high-holding power anchors are more effective than traditional types in sand, mud and clay and are the preferred choice of most yachtsmen.

Fisherman's and grapnel anchors work best on rock and coral. Because of the poorer holding in soft seabeds, they need to be heavier than high-holding anchors. Consequently, they will often hold well in sea grass and weed-strewn bottoms.

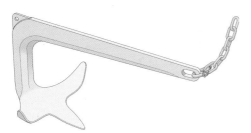

Bruce (Claw) – high holding power. Originally designed for holding North Sea oil rigs. Awkward to stow in a small anchor locker.

Delta – high holding-to-weight ratio. Relatively-low price, no moving parts. Designed to be stowed on bow roller for self launching.

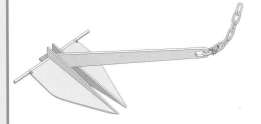

Danforth – Many similar styles (Meon). High holding-power-to-weight ratio. Stows flat. Digs in well to mud but can be hard to break out.

CQR (plough) – High holding-to-weight ratio. Popular but hard to stow.

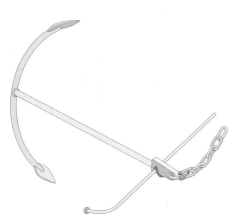

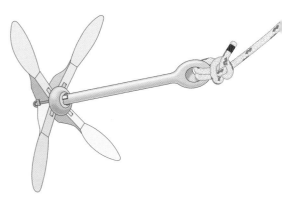

Fisherman's – traditional anchor, small fluke size provides poor holding in mud and sand. Good for rocky and weedy bottoms.

Grapnel – poor holding in mud and sand, better in rocks and weedy bottoms. Most allow the flukes to fold up along the shaft, held by a collar, for easy stowage.

What anchors do you need?

At least two anchors should be carried on a cruising boat – a bower and a kedge.

The bower is the boat's main anchor, used for overnight or longer stops, while the kedge is a lighter weight anchor used for shorter stays in good weather. Traditionally, the kedge was used for kedging a ship off the dock in the days when ships didn't have engines, or used to refloat when run aground. The kedge anchor was loaded into a dinghy, rowed away from the ship and dropped so that the ship could be pulled to the anchor. It was then free to get under way.

Today, in addition to short stops, the kedge anchor can be used for pulling a grounded boat off the sand or mud. However, it is often used as a second anchor in support of the main bower anchor. The table below is the MCA's requirements for the minimum size of conventional digging-type anchors and their cable. Vessels with high windage, such as tall motor cruisers and cruising catamarans, may have to increase anchor specification by at least 25%.

Mean Length (See note 4)	Anchor mass		Anchor cable diameter			
	Main	Kedge	Main Chain	Main Rope	Kedge Chain	Kedge Rope
(metres)	(kg)	(kg)	(mm)	(mm)	(mm)	(mm)
6	8	4	6	12	6	10
7	9	4	8	12	6	10
8	10	5	8	12	6	10
9	11	5	8	12	6	10
10	13	6	8	12	6	10
11	15	7	8	12	6	10
12	18	9	8	14	8	12
13	21	10	10	14	8	12
14	24	12	10	14	8	12
15	27	13	10	14	8	12
16	30	15	10	14	8	12
17	34	17	10	14	8	14
18	38	19	10	16	8	14
19	42	21	12	16	10	14
20	47	23	12	16	10	14
21	52	26	12	16	10	14
22	57	28	12	19	10	16
23	62	31	12	19	10	16
24	68	34	12	19	10	16

1. Chain cable diameter given is for short link chain. Chain cable should be sized in accordance with EN 24 565:1989 (covering ISO 4565: 1986 and covered by BS 7160:1990 - Anchor chains for small craft), or equivalent.
2. The rope diameter given is for nylon construction. When rope of another construction is proposed, the breaking load should be not less than that of the nylon rope specified in the table.
3. When anchors and cables are manufactured to imperial sizes, the metric equivalent of the anchor mass and the cable diameter should not be less than the table value.
4. For the purposes of this section, mean length is defined as: $\frac{\text{Length} + \text{Length on waterline}}{2}$

Anchor cable – chain or warp?

The choice between using all chain or a mixture of chain and warp usually depends on the size of the boat and what you use your boat for. Cruising-style boats that are frequently anchored for extended periods of time in a wide range of conditions will be better off using an all-chain rode, whereas a racing boat that anchors only occasionally and for short periods of time will use a mixture of chain and warp. All-chain rodes can be comfortably carried on larger boats, whereas on a smaller vessel an all-chain rode may affect the performance due to the additional weight. When it's possible to have the choice, all-chain is more efficient, length for length, than chain and warp.

Nylon rope is the best choice for the warp, due to its elasticity, ideally of multiplait construction.

The amount of rode to deploy will depend on the conditions and whether it's chain or chain and warp. As a rule of thumb the minimum to deploy is…

4 x depth of water at HW, when anchoring with chain

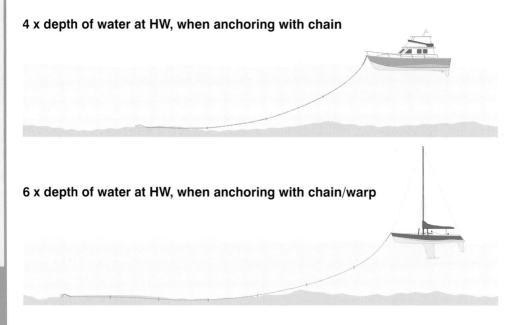

6 x depth of water at HW, when anchoring with chain/warp

In heavy weather, up to 10 times the depth or more may be needed.

If you use chain/warp, always have at least 5 metres or, if longer, the same length as the boat of chain. The chain is not only better able to withstand chafe as it drags across the seabed but also provides a better angle of pull on the anchor's stock. Ideally, the pull on to the anchor should be as close to horizontal as possible otherwise it reduces the anchor's holding power.

The bitter end (opposite end to anchor) of the warp should be attached to a strong point inside the chain locker. If all-chain then make fast the bitter end with a short length of rope – sufficient to reach the deck through the chain pipe – which can be buoyed and cut if the anchor needs to be released in an emergency.

The shackle between the chain and anchor should be secured either by securing the pin with seizing wire or peening the end of the shackle pin so that it cannot come undone. Stainless steel shackles are particularly prone to becoming undone.

If using an anchor windlass, it's advisable to replace the shackle with a strong swivel to prevent twist in the chain.

Regularly inspect the connection between chain and rope in chain/warp rodes. Multiplait rope can be easily spliced on to the chain for the strongest joint. Three-plait rope is best made into an eye around a galvanised or stainless

steel thimble and shackled to the chain. Three-plait rope joined direct to the chain will wear and can fail.

Mark the rode at regular intervals – say every five metres – so that it is easy to judge how much cable has been let out. If using cable ties, do not cut the ties since the sharp edges can easily cut hands. A pair of leather gardening gloves help to protect the hands when handling the warp.

CHAPTER
10

Deck fittings

Deck fittings need to be sturdy and strong since the loads imposed by the anchor and cable can be severe. The cable should be led over a bow roller, or fairlead, that can be closed over the cable to prevent it jumping out, as the boat pitches, and sawing into the boat's decks. Ideally, the boat should be fitted with a Samson post but sadly

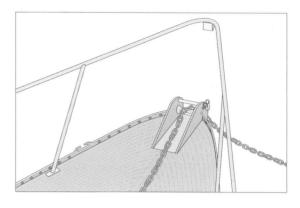

these are seldom seen on modern boats. In which case, attach the anchor cable to a strong cleat or cleats on the foredeck. The cleats must have large reinforcing backing plates under the deck.

In heavy weather, it may be necessary to spread the load over several foredeck cleats.

No bow roller or fairlead?

On sports boats, RIBs and other trailer boats where a bow roller is not fitted, it is often better to anchor from the stem eye. A painter (length of strong warp) should be attached to the stem eye when the boat is out of the water. The painter must be shorter than the length of the boat so that if it falls overboard it does not become entangled with the boat's propeller.

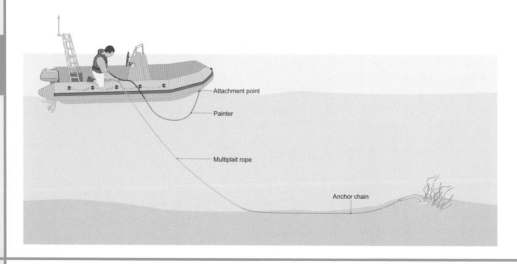

Attachment point

Painter

Multiplait rope

Anchor chain

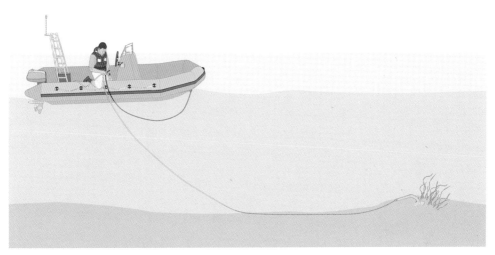

Lower the anchor over the side and pay out the required amount of anchor cable. Attach the painter to the anchor cable – a rolling hitch works well – and continue to let out more cable until the painter is pulling on the anchor cable.

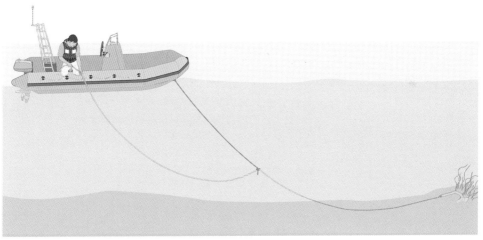

To recover the anchor simply pull in the anchor cable, untie the painter, and pull in the rest of the cable rode.

Anchor chum

To improve the angle of pull on the anchor, an anchor chum or angel can be lowered down the cable to increase the load in the middle of the catenary.

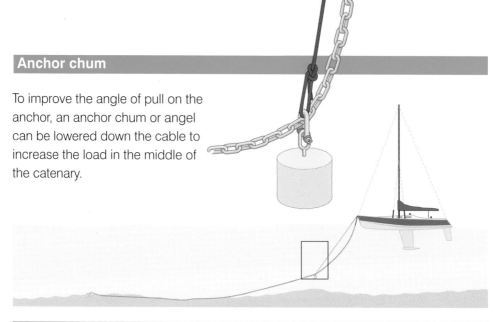

Sea anchors

In deep water, where a normal anchor wouldn't reach the bottom, a sea anchor will keep the bow head to wind and waves and reduce the chance of capsize or pitch-poling. They are particularly useful for catamarans and motor cruisers – that would turn their sterns towards the waves – but can be used on all types of craft. They are similar in size and shape to parachutes. A sea anchor for a 10-metre yacht would be about 4-metres in diameter.

As with a ground anchor, nylon warp or chain and warp will reduce snatching. The sea anchor should be deployed with sufficient length warp to ensure it stays submerged – at least 2 to 3 wave lengths and possibly as much as 100-metres of warp.

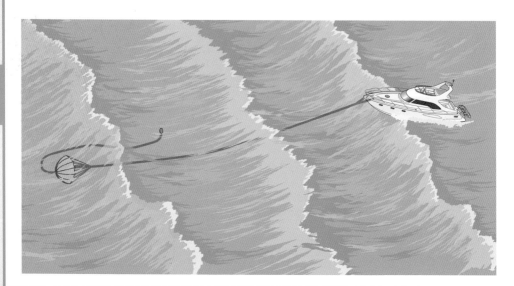

Drogues

To help prevent broaching when travelling with a following sea, deploy a drogue or trail a loop of long warp. A drogue is in effect a small version of a sea anchor.

Identify yourself

Make it easy for other boats and the SAR services to identify you by showing the boat's name on the side in large letters either on dodgers or on the mainsail cover – remember when the sails are up, the name is not visible. Sportsboats often have the name written in large letters on the boat's topsides.

If the name is too long use the boat's radio call sign.

Buckets and bilge pumps

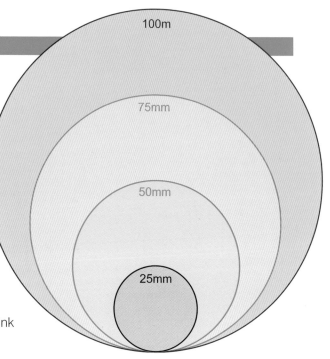

It's surprising just how much water can flood through a relatively small hole in the hull. The flow rate will depend on the size of the hole and the amount of head (depth below waterline). For example a 75mm (3 inch) hole less than a third of a metre (12 inches) beneath the waterline will let in 600 litres per minute – well over half a ton of water in a minute. A 25ft yacht weighing 2 tonnes would sink in three to four minutes.

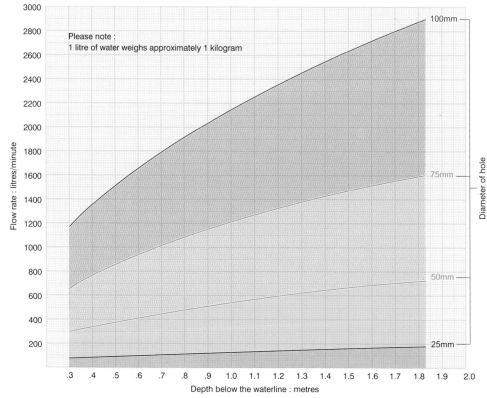

Rate of water ingress through 25, 50, 75 and 100mm holes at various depths

Please note :
1 litre of water weighs approximately 1 kilogram

Flow rate : litres/minute

Depth below the waterline : metres

Diameter of hole

Reducing the size of the hole, even by partially blocking it, will reduce the flow rate considerably. The aim is to reduce the flow to a level that bilge pumps and bailing can cope with.

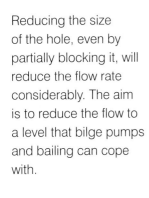

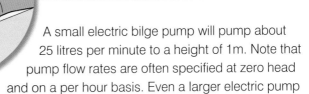

A small electric bilge pump will pump about 25 litres per minute to a height of 1m. Note that pump flow rates are often specified at zero head and on a per hour basis. Even a larger electric pump is unlikely to give more that 65 to 70 lt/minute. Clearly the hole will have to be reduced to less than 25mm (1 inch) diameter.

Electric pumps should not be relied on, not only because of their poor pumping rate but also because of their reliance on electrical power.

Manual pumps are more effective – for as long as you have the physical strength to pump. A small diaphragm pump should be capable of almost 40 lt/minute while larger pumps can provide over 100 lt/minute.

Diaphragm pumps are suitable for use as bilge pumps. Their simple construction make them easy and quick to service and remove blockages.

Whatever the pump, make sure they are fitted with a good strainer (strumbox) and that the bilges are kept clean. A matchstick can stop a pump from working.

At least one strong 10-litre bucket should be carried. Attach a lanyard to its handle so that it can be used either to collect water from the sea for fire fighting or thrown down into a cabin when bailing out. A panicking man with a bucket can shift a lot of water!

CHAPTER

10

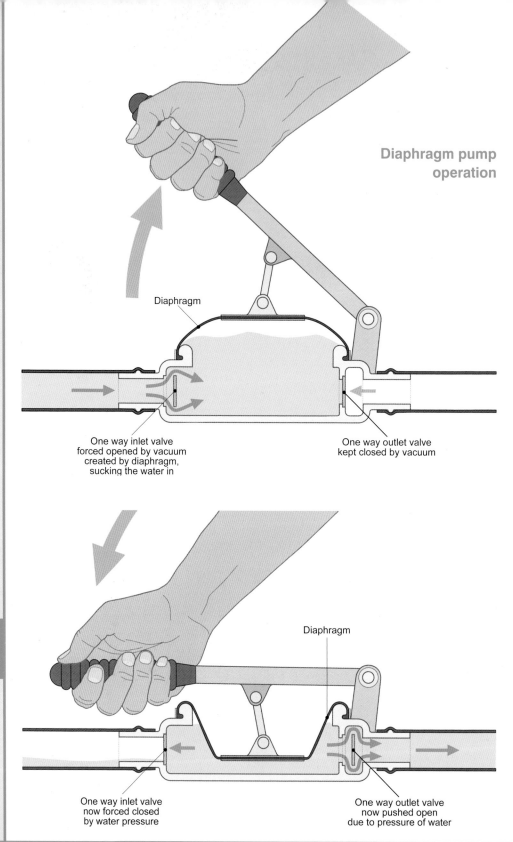

Diaphragm pump operation

Diaphragm

One way inlet valve
forced opened by vacuum
created by diaphragm,
sucking the water in

One way outlet valve
kept closed by vacuum

Diaphragm

One way inlet valve
now forced closed
by water pressure

One way outlet valve
now pushed open
due to pressure of water

CHAPTER
10

Temporary hull repair kit

Wooden bungs, of an appropriate size, should be attached to all underwater through hull fittings so that in the event of the fitting failing, due to corrosion or the hose coming off, the correct size bung is immediately available to plug the hole.

Seacocks must be well maintained and checked for use.

Underwater-curing epoxy repair kits are available to provide a rapid seal to cracks in glassfibre or wood.

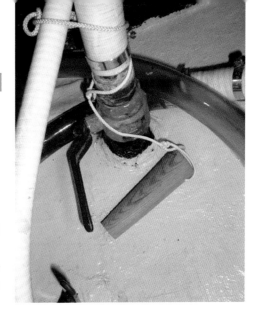

Washboards

To prevent down flooding if the cockpit is swamped because of a wave breaking into the cockpit or during capsize, make sure the washboards can be secured in place. The fastening must be able to be released from inside the cabin to allow crew to escape in an emergency. ISAF require this for most racing yacht categories.

Boat owners should consider how they would deal with a broken hatch whilst at sea. Boards which could be secured in place to prevent further water ingress should be considered.

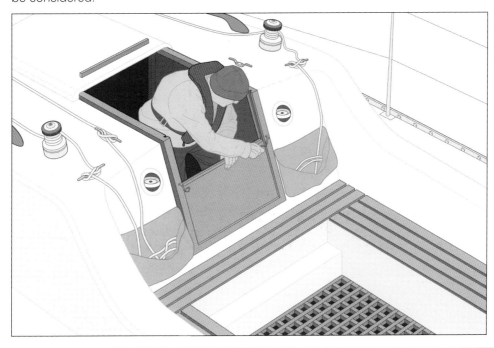

First aid kit

A suitable first aid kit and the knowledge to use it should be classed as on-board essentials. The first aid kit contents and level of ability required in administering first aid will vary for different types of boat and their usage. The kit and training should therefore be tailored to the level of self-sufficiency the nature of the boating will necessitate.

For short trips where help is readily at hand, a good quality first aid kit, as you would have at home, will suffice. For example, the kit will need sufficient dressings to stem bleeding until help arrives or the casualty can be taken ashore. A boating family will deal with individual needs such as indigestion tablets or antihistamine for allergies. Sea sickness remedies and sun protection are also important for boating.

This will of course only suffice if, in the event of an injury or illness which cannot be treated on board, the vessel is able to reach the shore quickly or request assistance with the evacuation of the casualty to the appropriate shore-side care easily achieved. Otherwise a more substantial first aid kit and additional first aid training will be needed.

Before you "cast off"

Skippers should ensure that they are aware of any medical problems their crew have or take medication for, ensuring they have enough medication with them. Both the skipper and the crew should be aware of any allergies or contra-indications among those on board in case of an emergency.

Crew should be briefed on potential dangers on board a boat prior to departure. On a sailing yacht, the boom, sheets and other trip hazards such as deck fittings, cleats, harness points, jack stays, winches and wet slippery decks are just a few of the dangers. On a fast moving motor yacht, any movement around the boat while it is on the plane can be hazardous and extreme caution is required.

Accidents will of course still happen and first aid equipment should therefore be available aboard all craft.

First Aid Manual

Knowing what is wrong with someone is of course the first step towards helping them. For this a first aid manual is invaluable and it is essential to carry one with you. The St John/ St Andrew's/Red Cross First Aid Manual as used during the RYA First Aid Course is recommended.

First Aid Courses

The first aid supplies are of course not much use without the knowledge to allow good use to be made of them. The RYA First Aid Course is designed for sailors venturing up to about 60 miles offshore and is taught by instructors with experience of teaching afloat. It covers the important first aid subjects from a specialist point of view. It also includes hypothermia, drowning, seasickness and dehydration, and how to get radio medical advice and the evacuation of a casualty by helicopter.

If the RYA course is not available try to find one that includes hypothermia and drowning. More information is available from RYA Training.

On all but the smallest boats, it is good practice to have two first aid kits on board, one for day to day use which your crew can help themselves from for regular requirements such as plasters, and a second which is reserved for incidents, so you do not find that something critical is missing at the most inopportune of moments.

Stowage and Maintenance

The first aid kit should be stored in a damp-proof strong canvas bag or box which is clearly labelled. Your first aid kit should not be forgotten in your maintenance routine, as medicines will go out of date. Check the contents and dates regularly and retain the instructions for all items.

Inshore

A very basic first aid kit will be needed for inshore boating: Sun cream and medication relative to the crew needs e.g. sea sickness tablets, headache tablets, asthma treatment, plus for minor accidents plasters, wound dressings, triangular bandages, gloves, and a thermal protective aid.

Coastal

Equipment: Gloves, thermal protective aid, triangular bandages, supporting (crepe) bandage, tough cut shears (for cutting clothing), tweezers, resuscitation pocket mask.
Medications: Sun cream, sea sickness tablets, paracetamol, ibuprofen, aspirin, antihistamine cream/tablets, indigestion tablets, Imodium® (or alternative diarrhoea remedy), rehydration salts, and medication relative to the crew needs e.g. asthma treatment.

Wounds: Plasters, wound dressings, antiseptic wipes, clingfilm, eye dressing.

First aid best practice and advice is continually changing and evolving. Taking up-to-date advice and tailoring the first aid kit to the individuals are both essential elements of voyage preparation.

Offshore and Ocean

The further offshore you go and the longer passages you undertake, the more you increase the need for self-sufficiency.

A medical history for the crew on board and advice from their doctor on the medicines required, storage conditions and any likely complications would be worth considering. In general you should think about whether you need to be equipped to deal with eye problems, allergic reactions, cold sores, thrush, severe pain, infections, dental problems, vomiting and diarrhoea, angina and more significant wounds.

A vessel operating commercially is required to carry certain drugs on board by the Merchant Shipping (Medical Stores) Regulations 1995, and is therefore able to obtain certain controlled drugs without a prescription. A private yachtsman is, however, effectively in the same position as a private individual ashore. Therefore, while drugs such as very strong painkillers and antibiotics may be desirable, such controlled drugs can only be obtained with a prescription from a qualified medical practitioner. Illegal possession could result in prosecution.

The training course *Medical First Aid Aboard Ships* is recommended for offshore passages and *Medical Care Aboard Ships* is recommended for ocean voyages. Although these are not RYA courses they are offered by some RYA Training Centres, where it is likely the course will be geared more towards yachts than ships.

The Ship's Captain's Medical Guide which supports these courses is another good reference book to have on board and MSN 1768, which details the items commercial vessels making such passages are required to carry, could be useful as background reading.

Depending on training, items carried might include:

Equipment: Gloves, thermal protective aid, triangular bandages, supporting (crepe) bandage, tough cut shears, tweezers, hot water bottle, splinting equipment, neck collar, needles and syringes, pocket mask for resuscitation, dental care kit, oxygen, defibrillator, suctioning equipment, suture kit, scalpel, forceps, thermometer, scissors, instrument cleaning kit, safe disposal equipment, cathetering equipment, stethoscope, hypothermic thermometer, blood pressure monitor, body bag.

Medications: Sun cream, sea sickness tablets, paracetamol, ibuprofen, aspirin, antihistamine cream/tablets, indigestion tablets, Imodium®, rehydration salts, sterile eye wash, anaesthetic eye drops, antibiotics, antibiotic cream, very strong painkillers, local anaesthetic, laxatives, cream for skin infections, anti-anxiety medication, eye antibiotic cream, haemorrhoid cream, ear drops, and medication relative to the crew needs e.g. asthma treatment, the treatment for anaphylaxis.

Wounds: Plasters, wound dressings, antiseptic wipes, clingfilm, eye dressing, wound closure strips, wound care kits, tubular gauze, paraffin gauze dressings, burn dressings, surgical tape, and sterile dressings.

Should it be necessary to top up the kit along the way anything obtained overseas should be clearly marked, as to what it is and what it is for, dosage required etc.

"Foreign" diseases

International travel advice should be followed, with necessary inoculations obtained and preventative treatments for diseases such as malaria obtained if recommended. For some countries, where disposable syringes and needles are not generally used, carrying a personal 'sharps' kit in case you need treatment in hospital can be advisable.

Cool weather clothing

It is always colder on the water than it is on land so you need to make sure you have the right clothing for the conditions. Take extra and spare clothing with you.

Synthetic materials are better at wicking moisture away from the skin. Breathable waterproofs keep you warmer not only by keeping you dry from the outside but also by reducing moisture created by your body from becoming trapped inside the clothing, which can make you feel wet and clammy.

Marine clothing manufacturers now provide layer systems that are better able to keep you comfortable in a range of weather conditions.

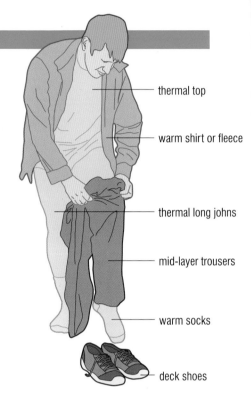

- thermal top
- warm shirt or fleece
- thermal long johns
- mid-layer trousers
- warm socks
- deck shoes

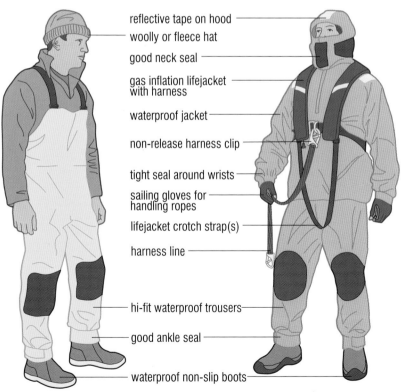

- reflective tape on hood
- woolly or fleece hat
- good neck seal
- gas inflation lifejacket with harness
- waterproof jacket
- non-release harness clip
- tight seal around wrists
- sailing gloves for handling ropes
- lifejacket crotch strap(s)
- harness line
- hi-fit waterproof trousers
- good ankle seal
- waterproof non-slip boots

Warm weather clothing

In hot weather, protect yourself from the sun. UV light is reflected by the sea and can increase the possibility of sunburn. Use sun block or high factor cream. Don't forget vulnerable areas such as the top of your feet and ears and the front of your legs. Long sleeve shirts and broad-brimmed hats give added protection while wrap-around sunglasses reduce glare.

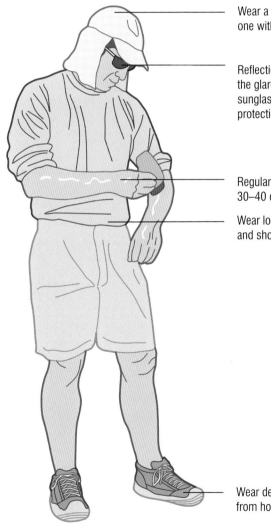

Wear a wide-brimmed hat or one with neck protection.

Reflection from water increases the glare effect of the sun. Use sunglasses with 100% UVA protection.

Regularly apply sunblock of SPF 30–40 on exposed skin.

Wear loose long sleeved shirts and shorts.

Wear deck shoes to protect feet from hot decks and stubbing toes.

CHAPTER
10

Immersion suits

If voyaging long distances or in coldwater areas, it makes sense to carry on board cold water immersion suits for every crew member. Indeed, since 2006, an immersion suit is required for every person on board a cargo vessel that operates in a cold-water area. They are bulky and, therefore, not easy to stow in the confines of a small boat.

There is a broad variety of types from thick neoprene insulated suits to those that are made from PU-coated nylon similar to diving drysuits and require insulated clothing to be worn beneath the suit. Both types usually have insulated hoods to minimise heat loss.

They require practice to be donned quickly.

Unless built-in buoyancy is provided, they should be worn with a 275N lifejacket to ensure sufficient buoyancy is available to turn and keep the wearer face up.

Emergency knife

Keep an emergency knife for cutting rope quickly in a handy place in the cockpit. Some crew carry their own knife so that they can cut their safety lanyard if it should become snagged or cause them to be dragged dangerously alongside the boat.

The emergency knife should have a blunt point and a serrated blade, which has been found to be the best for cutting rope.

> To stop the blade from corroding, wipe with candle wax to form a protective layer.

Multifunction tools can also be useful and usually include a serrated blade.

In the UK, it is generally an offence to carry a knife in a public place without good reason or lawful authority – this doesn't include pen knives with non-locking blades less than 3in in length. It is probably best to keep the knife aboard the boat or to keep secure in your luggage.

Drinking water

On a cruising boat, carry an emergency supply of drinking water that is separate from the main tank. Opaque plastic water containers are more algae resistant than clear ones. Renew the water regularly to avoid contamination. On longer passages you will want to carry an emergency supply of drinking water, the volume of which will be dictated by the length of your planned passage. In addition to this, many long-distance cruisers will elect to carry a hand-operated desalinator.

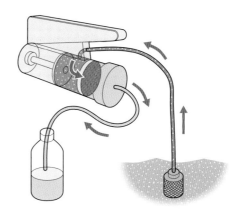

Using reverse osmosis, the desalinator can be used to make sea water drinkable by removing 98% of the salt. It can produce as much as 4 to 5 litres of drinking water per hour but is physically hard work to operate.

Emergency repair materials

Since help is not always close at hand when you are at sea, it makes sense to carry a variety of repair materials that can be used to cobble a repair to keep the boat going so that you can return to safety. Every skipper's list will be slightly different – to suit their boat – but here are some suggestions that might come in useful.

- Shackles
- Snatch block
- Duct tape
- Insulating tape
- Self-amalgamating rubber tape
- Selection of screws, nuts and bolts
- Lengths of rope and cord

- Hose clips
- Hose
- Wooden board (to cover broken hatches)
- Glassfibre repair materials
- Inflatable boat repair materials
- Epoxy putty
- Glue

Common sense

Don't forget a large helping of common sense. Never over estimate your ability, the ability of your crew or your boat. If you don't think it's safe to go out, don't go.

Chapter 11 Making Boating Safer

HMCG Voluntary Safety Identification Scheme – CG66

In the United Kingdom, the Coastguard run a free voluntary identification scheme that allows owners to register details of their craft on a national database for use in an emergency. The scheme ensures the CG Maritime Rescue Co-ordination Centres have a full description of your vessel, its likely cruising area and the safety and communications equipment on board. These details can be invaluable to the search and rescue services.

The owner can register his boat details either on a paper form, which is sent to the nearest MRCC, or, preferably, online via the MCA website.

Information, which can include a photograph of the vessel, is kept purely for SAR purposes and, to be kept 'active', must be updated every two years.

RNLI's free sea safety advice service

The Royal National Lifeboat Institution provides a free specialist safety advice service to all who go afloat for pleasure. The service is centred on volunteer Lifeboat Sea Safety Officers and teams of trained and experienced volunteer sea safety advisers who are based at Lifeboat stations. The volunteers can provide advice from how to wear and maintain a lifejacket correctly through to a thorough, in-depth and impartial assessment of your boat's safety equipment.

They run sea safety advice days and provide free safety presentations and demonstrations to clubs and associations.

They also have a free range of literature including Sea Safety: The Complete Guide booklet, which includes a comprehensive interactive CD-ROM that automatically updates when the user goes on-line.

For free advice or to arrange a presentation or demonstration or to ask for copies of their free literature contact the RNLI on 0800 328 0600 or visit their website www.rnli.org.uk/seasafety

RYA Tick mark

While many marine products are often made to a recognised standard, such as those published by the International Standards Organisation (ISO), many of the standards can be self-certified by the manufacturer/supplier.

Realising the potential pitfalls of a self-certification system, the RYA have used their RYA Tick mark scheme to show that a manufacturer's claim of meeting the ISO standard has been verified by a third party (the RYA).

The scheme has run for several years for boats – confirming builders' claims for stability and construction standards have been met – and, of course, as a sign that sea schools meet the RYA's training standards.

However, in 2008 the scheme was expanded to include safety equipment. The first safety equipment to be verified by the RYA to meet ISO 9650 is a range of liferafts from Ocean Safety.

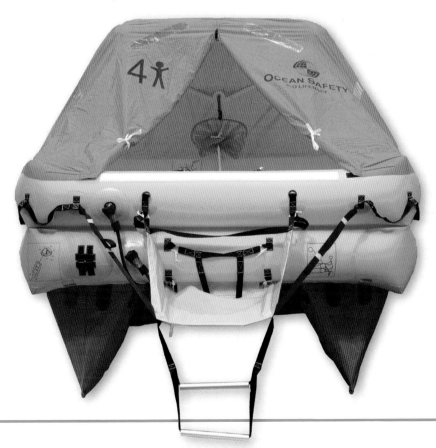

Learning from others' experience

Skippers of pleasure craft, being used for leisure purposes only, are not required to report accidents or near misses. However, voluntary reporting is recommended so that we can share experiences and hopefully prevent further accidents or dangerous incidents.

In the UK, there are three organisations that accept or investigate reports of incidents and accidents at sea.

Marine Accident Investigation Branch - MAIB

If an accident happens in UK waters or to a UK-registered vessel abroad, it is the Department of Transport's MAIB that investigates the accident to determine what went wrong and provide recommendations to prevent similar accidents in the future. They look into all major accidents, especially when there has been loss of life, of all types of vessel from large ships down to small sports boats and dinghies.

The reports are well worth reading. They are free and published quarterly on their website, and in print, and provide a detailed analysis of the incident and advice to prevent similar incidents for happening again.

Confidential Hazardous Information Reporting Programme - CHIRP

CHIRP is an independent and impartial confidential reporting programme for people employed or having an active interest in the maritime industry. Pleasure boaters can use CHIRP to highlight safety related issues or report hazardous incidents. Reports that are of use to a wider audience are published in their quarterly newsletter and on their website – **www.chirp.co.uk.**

All personal details are removed to ensure absolute confidentiality. The only people who have access to personal details are the staff at CHIRP dealing directly with the report. Comments made by CHIRP are reviewed by their Maritime Advisory Board, which has members from a wide range of maritime organisations.

Marine Accident Reporting Scheme - MARS

The Marine Accident Reporting Scheme is a confidential reporting system run by The Nautical Institute for reporting of accidents and near misses with shipping. The reports are published in 'Seaways' – the Institute's monthly journal. Reports are submitted direct to MARS using a step-by-step form on the MARS website.

USEFUL CONTACT DETAILS

RYA
RYA House
Ensign Way
Hamble
Hants
SO31 4YA
Tel: 02380 604 100
www.rya.org.uk

RNLI
West Quay Road
Poole
BH15 1HZ
Tel: 0845 0456999
www.rnli.org.uk

MCA
Maritime and Coastguard Agency
Spring Place
105 Commercial Road
Southampton
Hants
SO15 1EG
Tel: 02380 329 100
www.dft.gov.uk/mca

Small Ships Register
UK Ship Register - RSS
Anchor Court
Keen Road
Cardiff
CF24 5JW

Ofcom
Ofcom
Riverside House
2a Southwark Bridge Road
London
SE1 9HA
Tel: 020 7981 3040
www.ofcom.org.uk

ISAF
ISAF (UK) Ltd
Ariadne House
Town Quay
Southampton
Hampshire
SO14 2AQ
Tel: 02380 635 111
www.sailing.org

EPIRB Registration
The EPIRB Registry
Falmouth MRCC
Pendennis Point
Castle Drive
Falmouth
Cornwall
TR11 4WZ
Tel: 01326 211 569
Online registration: http://www.
dft.gov.uk/mca/mcga07-home/
emergencyresponse/mcga-
searchandrescue/epirb/mcga-sar-epirb-
online.htm

INDEX